T0157019

and you thought
accounting was boring

and you thought accounting was boring

or the debit is the side towards the window

EDWARD GOTBETTER, CPA

iUniverse, Inc.
Bloomington

and you thought accounting was boring
or the debit is the side towards the window

Copyright © 2011 by Edward Gotbetter, CPA.

All rights reserved. No part of this book may be used or reproduced by any means, graphic, electronic, or mechanical, including photocopying, recording, taping or by any information storage retrieval system without the written permission of the publisher except in the case of brief quotations embodied in critical articles and reviews.

iUniverse books may be ordered through booksellers or by contacting:

iUniverse
1663 Liberty Drive
Bloomington, IN 47403
www.iuniverse.com
1-800-Authors (1-800-288-4677)

Because of the dynamic nature of the Internet, any web addresses or links contained in this book may have changed since publication and may no longer be valid. The views expressed in this work are solely those of the author and do not necessarily reflect the views of the publisher, and the publisher hereby disclaims any responsibility for them.

Any people depicted in stock imagery provided by Thinkstock are models, and such images are being used for illustrative purposes only.
Certain stock imagery © Thinkstock.

ISBN: 978-1-4620-3536-6 (sc)
ISBN: 978-1-4620-3537-3 (ebk)

Printed in the United States of America

iUniverse rev. date: 08/01/2011

To our youngest daughter Marion who left this earth much too soon at the early age of 49. She was the spark that lit up a room whenever she entered. All who had the privilege to know and love her will forever miss her. Carmen, the love of her life, has remained with us as our daughter.

To Frances my wife and best friend who has enjoyed the good times we have had and the bad times that we have endured in our 63 years of marriage.

To our other two daughters Susan and Amy and their respective husbands Tom and Spencer who have all always looked out for our welfare.

To our fantastic grandchildren Danielle, her brother Dr. Joshua and his wife Faith. If we had known that they would be such a joy, we would have had them first.

To Patty Bashe Romanowski, my friend, client and editor. Her suggestions were more than well received and most appreciated.

In The Beginning

To say that I came from very humble beginnings would be to understate the history of my growing up. My mother came to this country from what was the Austrian Hungarian Empire under Franz Joseph. She came from a small town in what is now the Ukraine by the name of Zohkiev. It was a suburb of Lemberg, now called Lvov. Her uncle and aunt who had migrated to New York City in the late 1880s had sent a steamship ticket for my grandfather to come to New York City. The routine was at that time for the man to go New York, work hard and save money to enable him to send for his wife and children. My grandfather must have been a very religious and pious Jew and could not bring himself to go New York. However, one does not let a steamship ticket go to waste, so he sent my mother. This was 1913 and my mother was 13 years of age. They changed her papers to read that she was 16 so that she could travel by herself.

I cannot envision how a child of 13 could have travelled, all alone, by train to Rotterdam, boarded a ship and sailed off to America. Some adult must have helped her on the way. Of course she travelled in steerage and was sick most of the ocean journey. Her aunt and uncle were waiting for her at "Castle Gardens" in New York harbor. The year was 1913 as my mother was born in the year 1900.

She went to work immediately and worked as a servant for an optician who had a store on Lexington Avenue. One of her jobs took her to Pittsfield Massachusetts. She told me that for a while she had a job as someone who dipped cherries into chocolate. Even at this tender age, my mother was always hard working, a trait she would need to survive in the years to come.

Like all young women of her generation, she no doubt dreamed of marrying and raising a family. Somewhere she unfortunately met my father and he wooed her. Neither I, nor my sister, ever asked my mother how and where she met our father. I had heard that he had worked as a Western Union messenger. In those early days the New York City offices had a turn button on a wall to use when they wanted to send off a telegram. The bell would ring at the Western Union office and off my father would go to retrieve the message. One of the offices he called upon was the Bristol City Lines. They were located at One Broadway. They occupied offices on the top floor of the building. Their windows were portholes and they looked out upon the lower New York harbor and the Statue of Liberty. They were an English company, based in Bristol. They owned about a dozen cargo ships. My father had flaming red hair and must have made an impression on the manager of the New York office. He was supposedly asked how much he was earning at Western Union, or so he told me. He was probably making $3 or $4 a week and was offered a job for some increased figure. He accepted the job and worked there for the rest of his life.

My father was either patriotic, adventurous, a nut or wanting to make an impression on his bosses. Instead of waiting for the United States to enter the First World War, he went to Canada and enlisted in the Canadian Jewish Brigade. He was sent off to fight the Turks in Palestine. He was there until sometime in 1919. He had fought alongside General Allenby and David Ben Gurion. He had corresponded with my mother and when he returned he married my mother in 1920. My father bitched and complained all of his life that the British government had never given him any veteran's bonus or pension as the U. S. government had done for their veterans.

They were married for 11 years, when in January 1931 he packed a bag and walked out the door. People say that they remember things going back to their early childhood. I cannot remember a single event prior to me standing in the hallway of our apartment at 1735 Fulton Avenue in the Bronx, with my 9 year-old sister, Pearl, and my mother. I was only 6 and a half. It's ironic that I would grow up to care so little for the man whose decision that day so influenced the course of my life. Whatever sadness or loss I have felt for him would quickly be replaced by ambivalence, to say the least. I know that nowadays, with separations and divorces so common, it may be hard to understand just how devastating my father's departure was for our family. As harsh as it might sound, I have to be honest: it would have been better if my father had died. At least I would have fond memories of a loving father.

1735 Fulton Avenue was located in the South Bronx, bordering on Crotona Park and very close to the famous Bathgate Avenue, which was known for its outdoor market and pushcarts. One block to the right of our apartment house was Public School number 4. I attended kindergarten and first grade there and I think the school is still in operation.

Separations and divorces were not very popular in the 1930s. People stupidly wanted to know what my mother had done to make him walk out.

She had done nothing except marry the wrong man. He never admitted it but we knew that he had gone to live with his mistress.

Strangely, my parents never got divorced. Deeply in her heart, my mother long held out hope that my father would return to us, but he never did. My father was too shrewd to request a divorce because that would have entailed that he and my mother obtain attorneys and go to court. Under those circumstances my mother would have received more in alimony and child support than the paltry $10 a week that he gave us. Every other Saturday at noon, Pearl and I stood at the corner of Ward and Watson avenues. My father would drive up in a car that he would say he didn't own but had borrowed from a friend. He would hand us $20 and drive away.

He died at the age of 91 from lung cancer. He had been a very heavy smoker. On the rare occasions when I would visit him at his office at One Broadway, I would find him talking on the phone with a cigarette burning in his mouth. There would be one still burning in the ashtray and he reaching for another to light. When he died, we were sent his personal effects, after the staff at the nursing home had stolen his collection of silver dollars and other valuables. His effects, for some crazy reason contained all the car registrations for all the autos he had owned since the early 1930s.

I was in desperate need of a new pair of shoes and my mother pleaded with me to ask my father for another $3. I mustered up my courage after several weeks and asked him for the funds. He told me that he could not afford to give me any money. This was the height of the depression. The three of us were living in a two-room apartment paying $28 a month rent. Many people living in our apartment house were out of work and living on home relief as welfare was called in those days. The women would watch for the postman on the day that the payment would arrive and ask him for the check rather than have their neighbors know that they were poor. We never applied for home relief because we were both ashamed of the stigma and did not know if based on what we were receiving from my father if we would be entitled to any money. My mother never tried going to work and stayed at home to care for her children.

My father worked at his job all through the depression and I am certain that he was receiving a handsome salary. He was supporting two families and also had to give his parents some funds from time to time. His parents lived on Kelly Street in the Bronx. That was the same street on which General Colin Powell had resided.

I saw Colin Powell having lunch with his wife and another lady in the "Candy Kitchen" in Bridgehampton several months ago. I struck up a conversation with him and discussed my grandparents and Kelly Street. His aunt had lived in the same building with my grandparents and he lived down the block. He wanted to know which apartment my grandparents lived in. He was very kind and friendly.

We might have had some help from my father's parents, my grandparents, who lived nearby: at the very least, Pearl and I might have continued to see them and continued some semblance of the family we had known before my father abandoned us. Unfortunately my grandparents decided that we could no longer visit their apartment on Kelly Street, since they felt they had to "side" with their son and they didn't want to chance his becoming upset if he learned we had been there. Ironically the husband of their oldest daughter Fanny had deserted her and her three sons and they cursed him every day.

Interestingly, my mother did stay in contact with my father's younger brother, my uncle Abe and his wife Rosa. Abe was very bright: he graduated from high school at fifteen and from college four years later. He became both a certified public account and an attorney. My father got Abe a job working for Bristol City Lines and my father always contended that he covered for Abe on the job and let Abe study during the day. Abe's wife tante (aunt) Rosa towered over him, and together they had two sons. Rosa's father had a kosher butcher shop on Staten Island and we visited there on rare occasions.

I was fortunate to have Benny, my mother's cousin, in my life. He was a CPA, who worked for the Internal Revenue Service. Having graduated college at the height of the Depression, Benny found the only job available was with the IRS. He was sent to Chicago for about five years before being transferred back to New York. Since he was the intelligent one in our family, I have always resented that he did not do more to aid my mother with advice and direction in dealing with my father. Perhaps he did and my mother told him to forget it, but I do not think so.

4

As a result of the poverty and penny pinching life that my mother, sister and I lived in, I always felt that I had to do something to earn a few dollars and help out the family. As long as I can remember, I worked starting when I was about 9 years old. And when I say "work" I mean hard, difficult labor of a type that few adults these days, much less children, ever experience. After school, I went straight to work, doing my best to earn whatever little money I could. I approached every store in the neighborhood and offered my services. Obviously, I had no skills to speak of, but I quickly acquired a wealth of experience and soon learned the true value of a dollar. I was not shy or bashful when it came to approaching a prospective employer. For example, I worked in the "wet wash hand laundry", the drug store, the clothing cleaning store, and the grocery store, cleaning the dentist's office and cleaning the printing presses in the local printing stop.

At the hand laundry, I got up early and picked up dirty clothing to be washed and possibly ironed. In the afternoon, after school hours I would deliver the clean, wet laundry, which now weighed three times more than when I picked up the sack in the morning. I must have been all of ten years old. It was exhausting work. I usually asked the women if I would get a tip before schlepping the bags up the stairs. My goal was to collect as many tips as I could. Women would then hang the wet laundry on the clotheslines that crisscrossed courtyards and back alleys to dry. There were men who earned a living stringing these clotheslines for the house wives. Sometimes I stayed at the shop to iron sheets, pillowcases and other items in the mangle a large machine that pressed the fabric between two heavy very hot rollers. You had to be extremely careful not to let your fingers get too close to the hot metal plate at the top of the rollers.

At the drug store I wrapped Kotex and Modess boxes in plain brown paper so that no one would be able to read the labels (though in those days of course, everyone knew what was inside). Among my other jobs were grinding medicines with a mortar and pestle and pour liquid medicine from the large jugs it came in, to smaller bottles for sale. I delivered prescriptions and of course counted on getting tips. A nickel was the usual gratuity and I was glad to receive it.

The cleaning store only needed me to deliver the cleaned garments. At the grocery store, I would deliver groceries, arrange the inventory, candled eggs and learned to cut butter from a large keg into quarter pound slabs. For those of you who have never seen eggs candled, I can explain that you held up each egg before a light and you could see the inside of the egg. If there were a blood spot in the egg or other flaw it would be thrown away as unsalable. Another job had me working for a dentist; cleaning his office entailed sweeping, vacuuming and wiping down all the equipment. The dentist had three pump organs in his apartment that was adjacent to his office in the same suite. To play any of them, he needed someone to pump the air that carried the sound, and that was yet another of the many jobs that made up a quite diverse resume by the time I was in my teens.

Although every one of my jobs had its downsides, none beat my time working for a printer, where I had to remove ink from the printing plates and every other surface. As with my other jobs, I made no more than two or three dollars a week in wages, and maybe a bit more in tips. But my mother always let me know that she appreciated my contribution to the family. And I was proud of being able to help. Childhood was different then, especially during the Depression. Many of the luxuries of free time and play children expect today, most of us didn't even have time to think about. It was a different world.

My mother led a miserable life and I just wish I had prospered earlier in my life so that I might have given her some pleasures to which she was very much entitled. She was a kind, sweet wonderful lady. She lived by the creed that if you cannot say anything good about another person, then do not say anything.

When my sister married in December 1941, my brother in law Julius Brodinsky moved in with us and we all lived in the same apartment. We moved to a larger apartment on Morrison Avenue, just three blocks from where we resided previously. He and I went off to war early 1943 and I am certain that my mother and sister worried about us surviving for the next three years I served in the 283rd Engineer Combat Battalion. I was in the army for 37 months, two weeks, three days, four hours, three minutes and twelve seconds, but who was counting.

My mother did not enjoy good health. She had detached retinas in both eyes and lost most of her vision. She had a gall bladder operation while I was overseas and never mentioned it to me until I came home from Europe because she did not want me to worry about her.

I had sent home an allotment to my mother from my army pay each month.

She never used a penny of it and accumulated it in a saving account. When I married she gave me $2,300 as a wedding gift.

She developed cancer and passed away at the age of 61. While she was dying she told me to see to it that my father should not be allowed to come to her funeral. He was standing out in the hallway in the hospital waiting to find out her condition when I told him her request. He was shocked but since he had no choice, he did not come to her funeral.

The worst blow that befell my mother is when she found out after the war ended that her father, mother, four sisters, their husbands and an unknown number of nieces and nephews were all killed by the Nazis.

My father's girl friend must have died also from cancer. After my mother died he took up with a first cousin of his who was widowed. They got married soon afterward. I had no desire to attend the wedding. My sister who longed for my father's affection and wanted to establish a relationship with his new wife's children asked me to attend, which my wife and I did.

He and his new wife moved to Florida and bought a small house. He found out shortly after they were married that she suffered from mental problems and took huge doses of medication. She did not survive very long and her children came to visit to claim their inheritance. I understand that my father threw rocks at their car. He sold the house and took up with another widow in Florida. My father was a real Don Juan. This woman sold her house and moved back to her previous home in Petersburg, Virginia. I can only assume that the woman told him that if my father was in the neighborhood, he should stop by and say hello. He did better than that and went there to move in with her. He became ill and was hospitalized unbeknownst to me. One evening I received a phone call from a woman. She told me that she lived in New York and was the daughter of the women living in Petersburg. She also told me that my father cannot come back to live with her mother when he gets out of the hospital. I thanked her for the call and told her that I have no relationship with my father and I could not care less what he did when he gets of the hospital and hung up the phone.

My father was very self-sufficient. He contacted Social Services and made arrangement to move into a small apartment in Richmond. He developed lung cancer and was moved to an adjoining nursing home facility. He had a paper pasted to the back of his front door stating that he wanted to be barbequed upon his demise.

After visiting Williamsburg in the summer of 1990, my wife and I stopped off to see him in Richmond. It was the last time I saw him. When he died at the age of 91, I was called to see if I wanted to honor his wishes to be cremated. I told them to go ahead. After that my wife received a notice that there was a package at the post office for us. She went there and picked up the cremains of my father. I went fishing some time after that and threw the container overboard. It did not sink and I had to pull it back in and break open the carton and sprinkle the ashes.

My father worked at the same job all his life, as I said previously He worked his way up to the point where he made the decision as to how the cargo ship was to be loaded. He decided where to place the corrosives, perishables, flammables, etc. in the hold of the ship or on deck. The ship's captain would visit with my father at the last minute to perhaps make some minor adjustments. He never became the manager of the New York office. The company would send a new manager from England to replace the retiring or deceased former manager.

During the Second World War my father became a member of the British Ministry of Shipping. When I came home from Bremen, Germany March 1946, my father was able to determine the ship I was on, when it would arrive in New York and at which pier. He picked up my mother at 3 AM and when I walked down the gangplank he and my mother were waiting for me. Of the 3,000 men on the ship, I was the only one who had parents waiting for him.

Unlike most of the youngsters of today who complete high school go on to college and have no idea what they want to do with their lives, I have always wanted to be an accountant as far back as I can remember. I was an excellent mathematics student and concentrated my studies on those subjects I enjoyed. My father's brother Abe and my mother's cousin Benny were both Certified Public Accountants but I never consulted with either or them to discuss my future.

Even while attending high school at James Monroe in the Bronx from September 1938 to June 1941, I knew I wanted to pursue an accounting career. I was in the Honor School in high school that meant that I traveled through all the classes with the same twenty-three other students, seven boys and sixteen girls. We were not entitled to take any "commercial" courses such as bookkeeping, typing or stenography. I knew I wanted to learn bookkeeping and typing and so went to see the Honor School grade advisor and submitted my request. She was not delighted with my request but caved in when I explained my reasons for it. She allowed me to go with the students taking a "commercial" course and learn bookkeeping and typing but that precluded me from taking a second foreign language, which suited me, just fine. I still regret not having learned shorthand because it would have been a great aid in taking notes in the classroom and other situations. I still come home and have my wife tell me that I had received one or more phone calls and the messages are on the counter next to the phone. Of course, she recorded the messages in shorthand and has to read the messages to me. Most people do not know that Billy Rose, the man who created extravagances, won the world's championship in shorthand. He had broken his hand just before the competition but would not be deterred. He taped a potato into the palm of his hand and stuck a pencil into the potato and won the contest.

Of all the friends I had while growing up and going to high school, I and my friend Lenny were the only ones who went on the college. He had joined me in taking courses in bookkeeping and typing. I never thought of going anywhere other than City College Downtown. Back in 1941 there was no Baruch College. If my memory serves me, I think I had to have a high average of the high school grades and also take an entrance exam. There was absolutely no tuition. The only costs were to purchase books for each course. Rarely did I have to buy a new book. The students assembled on the ground floor of the school and bought and sold used books to each other. Occasionally a professor would write a new book or update a textbook he had written previously. That would require purchasing a new textbook much to my chagrin and my pocketbook.

While attending James Monroe High School, I became interested in photography. Our history teacher, Mr. Shapiro, was in charge of the photography club after school hours. He took the picture of me in his classroom. It must have been taken September 1937, shortly after my bar mitzvah. Note the Waterman pen, which disappeared shortly thereafter. Note also the ragged cuffs on my shirt, poverty personified. I remember Mr. Shapiro inviting the entire class to his home for a celebration. He was what a teacher should be.

I had a number of friends from the neighborhood with whom I remained close for many, many years. When I was in high school, once a week at night I used to go to a poolroom where cousin Izzy and his friends spent the evening shooting pool. The poolroom was located on West 167 Street. It was on the second floor of a dingy building and a typical pool hall. They would pay me for racking up the balls after each round. One night Izzy asked if I wanted to come down to his shop after school and work for him. I jumped at the chance to earn 30 cents an hour. Izzy had opened a small shop, in Manhattan on 25th Street between Broadway and 6th Avenue, manufacturing renewable commercial fuses after parting ways with Mike Wein. I would leave James Monroe about 1 PM; jump on the Lexington Avenue subway (now known as the number 6 line) at Elder Avenue for a nickel and head for work for a few hours each day.

Izzy, my mother's cousin Benny's younger brother had worked for an electrical distributor Gallant and Wein, who are still in business. Both Manny Gallant and Mike Wein were from the same town in Europe as my mother and were like family. One hot summer night, Manny scooped up a bunch of kids, including me, and took us to Starlight Park on the Bronx River. Originally built for the 1918 Bronx International Exposition of Science, Arts and Industries, it featured a roller coaster, swimming pool, circuses, and a 15,000-seat stadium that was home to the New York Giants soccer team (who knew?). There were free opera concerts and big band dance concerts.

Manny helped each of us into the small airplanes that "flew" through the air suspended on chains from a revolving central pillar. The ride was on an upper level. Unfortunately, the man in charge of the ride started it before Manny had a chance to return to the ground. He was struck in the head, fell off the platform, and subsequently died. When Mrs. Lilly Gallant sued the Starlight Park, I was called as a witness. I remember the principal, Mr. Maguire, at Herman Ridder Junior High calling me into his office, after he received a subpoena for me to testify. He gently lectured me on the importance of telling the truth as I remembered it. Mrs. Gallant won the suit, but never collected a nickel as Starlight Park went out of business.

Herman Ridder Junior High School was located on Boston Road and 173rd Street. It was practically new when I attended there from September 1936 to June 1938. The school had some very progressive ideas, one of which was that all the students had to learn to print manuscript rather than cursive writing. To this day I print everything I write and only use cursive writing to sign my name. Unfortunately the neighborhood has changed so much from the time that I attended Herman Ridder, that when my classmates wanted to arrange a reunion at the school, the police turned down our application.

After things quieted down, Izzy went to speak to Mike Wein about replacing Manny Gallant as co-owner. He was turned down and quit to start his own business, which was the luckiest thing that could have happened to him.

I attended James Monroe High School, on Boynton Avenue in the Soundview section of the Bronx. At the time, it was relatively new, having just been built in 1924. In those days, students were "tracked" into either a commercial or an academic course of study. There were two Honor Classes in each grade but we did mix much with the other class. Some of boys and girls in my class were absolutely brilliant. I have lost touch with them, but I am certain that some of them went on to do great things in law, science and medicine. The U. S. economy still had not recovered from the Great Depression, and times were hard for most of us. Sure, we could dream of going to college and pursuing more academic interests, but I was always practical. I set my sights on graduating high school with solid practical skills that would get me a job. Like many New York City public high schools James Monroe eventually succumbed to decades of general decline in the neighborhood. When I attended, it was considered a fine school, a shining gateway to the American dream for thousands of children of immigrants just like me. Alumni include baseball Hall of Fame member Hank Greenberg (who graduated a few years before I did), Pulitzer Prize winning cartoonist Jules Feiffer, and several famous actors, musicians, academics, politicians and a Nobel Laureate.

The grade advisor called me to task one day for not participating in the after school service organizations. I explained that I had to work and it was necessary for me to leave school as quickly as possible each day.

I worked in the machine shop until one-day cousin Benny who owned a part of Izzy's business, had a discussion with me and learned that I was studying bookkeeping. He let me begin to work on the books and keep track of the accounts receivable and payables.

I entered City College Downtown now known as Baruch College, September 1941 and continued to work for cousin Izzy and worked full time during the summer. While working for Izzy I obtained a job for my long time friend Lenny Fialkow, who because of his skinny appearance was nicknamed by our fellow workers as "muscles". One of the workers in the shop, we were only four at that time, got in touch with the electrical union and attempted to organize the shop. One day as I was leaving City College on 23rd Street a man, no taller than five feet, came up to me and asked if I was Eddie Gotbetter. I told him I was and he asked how I was going to vote concerning the union. I asked him if I had a choice and all he did was shake his head from side to side. When I got to work I related the incident to my cousin and he told me to vote for the union because he was going to move to New Jersey shortly. So at the age of eighteen I became a member of Local 3 International Brotherhood of Electrical Workers.

I got drafted February 1943. I was honorably discharged as a Master Sergeant. I had passed the examination to become a Warrant Officer but never went to be commissioned because I was afraid that I would have to remain in service for a longer period. During the time I was in service, I would receive mail from the union telling they were concerned with my welfare, would send me to school upon my return and would attempt to find work for me. I always thought that was very nice on their part and maybe I should have gone on to become a licensed electrician. I know the benefits would have been good.

While in the army I had taken an aptitude test and the result came back that I would make a good radio mechanic. At that time I was in the Army Air Corp. I told the interviewer that I had started college and wanted to be an accountant not a radio mechanic. I asked to be sent to army air force administration school, become a company clerk and then be stationed at an airfield. The officer told me that he would write down my request but I would never get clearance by the officer standing at the near door. So, I did the next best thing and went through another door and it worked. I was sent to Arkansas State College in Jonesboro, Arkansas.

Again my future took a turn away from accounting. Six weeks through the eight-week course to completion and assignment to an airfield I was called into the Captain's office. He asked me if I was interested in joining the new Army Specialized Training Program to study engineering. It was a new program to send servicemen back to college. I told him that I was not interested and was looking forward to becoming a company clerk. He said OK but the next morning I received orders to join the program. I asked the captain "what happened?" He said he had to fill a quota with men with an IQ in excess of 130 and I was the only one to fit the bill.

So, off I went to LSU in Baton Rouge, Louisiana to spend five weeks in blistering heat and humidity at what was called a STAR unit awaiting assignment. I was then transferred to Penn State University to study of all things electrical engineering.

While at Penn State I roomed with a fellow soldier from Brooklyn, Robert Gerber, who had attended NYU wanting to become a doctor. An opportunity, presented itself for him. The army was giving a test to qualify for the army to send you to medical school. He was most anxious to take the exam and insisted that I take it as well. It sounded like fun and I had nothing to lose. The exam was fascinating. I do not know why, but two parts of the exam have always stuck in my memory. One part was an open book exam question about how twins are formed at birth. Another part was one in which you were given a cut out profile of the face, which listed every muscle, blood vessel and tissue. You were allowed to study the picture for a period of time and then it was taken away. You were then given the same picture completely blank and were told to fill in all the components you could recall.

Out of a total score of 300 I scored 288 while Bob got 248. He was devastated but we had to appear before a three-man panel for a final review. The panel consisted of a doctor, an army doctor and an officer. If I had told them that I had always wanted to be a doctor but was too poor to even think about it, I am sure they would have accepted me. Instead I told the truth and told them that I might be interested in going to medical school and then go into research but I would not be interested in making house calls. They all jumped on me and told me that I was not really interested in becoming a doctor. Can you imagine that rejection-taking place today?

Robert talked his way into medical school and off he went to Albany Medical School. We corresponded regularly while I went to Europe and he went to medical school. The minute the war was over and I had survived, I never heard from him again

The photograph of me in uniform was taken while I was stationed at Penn State. I was 19 years old at the time.

The ASTP program came to an abrupt end in the spring of 1944. The army decided that we had a war to win. I was placed in the 95th Infantry Division at Indiantown Gap, Pennsylvania as an infantry rifleman and was about to go overseas with them until the commanding officer Major General Twaddle decided he did not want any ex air force men in his outfit. He would not send us back to the air force but shipped us off to Camp Butner, North Carolina to join the 283rd Engineer Combat Battalion. We went off to Europe shortly after D-Day and stayed as the army of occupation until March 1946.

There is no telling how lucky I was that I was not allowed to stay with the 95th Infantry Division. They were immediately sent to France with many ASTP men. They got into a terrible battle at Strasbourg, France and lost many men. A friend of mine from James Monroe High School, named Harry Baron, died in that battle.

I am not describing my entire 37 months in the service of the US Army because I have already written in detail my entire experience and have given copies to each of my children.

However, two episodes that occurred while in service bear mentioning at this point. I shipped off to Europe early in September 1944—well after D Day on June 6th. We were supposed to go directly to France, but were diverted to Liverpool, England. We took additional training for the next four months. I never want to see a brussels sprout again. I went on a 48-hour pass Christmas weekend with a friend from Delaware. He was a very handsome guy and could have been a movie star. We went to a USO dance in Manchester. We struck up a conversation with a lovely young lady. She asked me, a pimply skinny kid, to dance. While we were dancing she asked me if I spoke Chinese. I said what are you talking about? She then asked if I would like to go home with her for "gefilte fish." Obviously she was a Jewess and spotted me for a fellow tribesman.

At that time the English money was 12 pence to a shilling and 20 shillings to the pound. She changed the pound that I had and I gave my mate 10 shillings and told him that I would meet him at noon the next day to go back to camp together. We took a bus to her home where I met her mother and her brother. She enjoyed a delicious meal and when it came time to retire, I joined her brother in his bedroom.

Sometime during the night V bombs started dropping in the neighborhood. We all dressed and the brother suggested that we head for the air raid shelter. We got about 15 feet from the front door when a bomb exploded nearby and the front door rattled. The brother, in typical British humor laughed and said that was no sense leaving the house. The next morning we discovered that the house next door had been blown to bits.

I thanked the family for their hospitality and returned to the USO center. I will never forget what waited for me at the center. There was a notice posted on the bulletin board, which read "All men from shipping order 2054 C return to camp immediately." I called the camp and was told to return now.

When I left the camp there were about 50,000 men stationed there and when I got back to camp, it was completely deserted. Someone had packed my duffel bag and placed my rifle and helmet on top of the bag.

The entire camp had been called out the previous evening, Christmas Eve, to be shipped to the continent to aid in the Battle of The Bulge. MPs had been sent to every pub, dance hall and every other place they could think of to round up our unit. Obviously they had not located me. The 283rd Engineer Battalion was shipped off to Southampton for the voyage across the English Channel.

After returning to camp and awaiting orders, several other men drifted in who had not been located. One of our trucks arrived with two officers and a truckload of Bangalore torpedoes. They had been to a school to learn how to operate the torpedoes. Bangalore torpedoes are six-foot lengths of pipe loaded with explosives and are used to blow holes in barbed wire and hedgerows so that the infantry can advance. We climbed into the back of the truck and headed off to Southampton. I celebrated New Year Eve wandering around the town freezing to death.

We were then put onto a ship with our truck and were told we were on a ship carrying mail and would go right into Le Havre. Well, it took us 6 days to cross the channel. They just did not have a place for us to dock and we sat inside the submarine nets just waiting.

Once we got to shore, our officers went to find out where our battalion was located. They could get absolutely no information. One of the officers was related to a general who was currently at Verdun. We drove to Verdun and he went to see the general. He returned in about an hour with tears streaming down his face. He told us that our outfit had been sunk by a German submarine and most of the men were lost at sea. We were given two choices, one was to stay there and become MPs or we could go to find the remnants of our battalion. Of course we chose the latter. Our officer was a "genius". They had given him the name of the town where our battalion was located. Well, just as we have the same name of a city in more than one state here in the United States, the same situation exists in France.

We drove south to almost the Spanish border only to find that they had never even seen an American soldier. They consulted the map again and found that the name of the town they were seeking was also in Brittany.

The winter of 1944 was one of the coldest in European history and we nearly froze to death. We stopped one evening in the town of Ouzier Le Marche in Loir et Cher. The townspeople took excellent care of us, served us hot red wine from a samovar. We gave them some of our rations and they embellished them with sauces and it was delicious.

The mayor of the town invited the two officers to stay at his home. They did not speak a word of French and asked me to go with them since I had studied French. I became very friendly with the mayor M. Marcel Heron and corresponded with him for years until his demise. My daughter Susan spent a semester in Paris and went to visit M. Heron. She speaks French fluently. He was already in the hospital at that time. Susan must have asked someone which of the men in the room is M. Heron. When she was told, she entered the room and greeted M. Heron. He said, "Oh you recognized me." He died shortly thereafter.

We finally arrived at Chateaubriand and located our boys. It turned out that they were scheduled to sail on the Leopoldville, the ship that was torpedoed, but they had arrived too late in Southampton and sailed on other ships.

They were replacing the 800 men who had died in the incident and we were now part of the 66th Infantry Division. We were surrounding 50,000 Germans left behind in the Lorient Sector. News of the Leopodville disaster remained a top secret for many years.

The only claim to fame that we had was when we moved on to Germany. We were stationed in the town of Frechen, which is a few miles west of Cologne. We were called upon to construct a pontoon bridge, under fire, across the Rhine River north of Cologne. The only bridge across the Rhine that was captured in tact was the bridge at Remagen. It was captured by the 9th Armored Division but could not be used very long to cross the river because it had been damaged . . .

Captain Victor Vega stepped on a land mine on the east side of the river and we named the bridge after him. He lost a leg and gangrene set in. He was flown back to the states and survived.

The war ended May 8, 1945 in Europe and August 15, 1945 in Asia after the Atom Bomb was dropped on Japan. I remained in Germany in the army of occupation in Bavaria. Since I knew some Yiddush, I was able to adapt to the German spoken in Bavaria which is Platte Deutch. I did so well that one night we stopped a German who was out after curfew and he accused me of being a German working for the Americans because of the way I spoke German. We built the prisoner of war stockade in Nuremberg for the prisoners to be tried for crimes against humanity.

One of the most memorable events I had was not fighting in the war but attending a USO show in Bayreuth Germany. Bayreuth is a town that is famous because it is the birthplace of Wagner the composer of operas. The theatre has annual opera fests of his famous operas. Oddly enough, my son in law Tom, who loves Wagnerian operas, went to Bayreuth a couple of years ago to listen to the Ring (Wagner's famous operas).

On July 5, 1945 we heard of a USO show at the Bayreuth theatre. At that point I was a Master Sergeant and was allowed to take a huge truck and drive about 50 miles to Bayreuth with about 40 men in the back of the truck. I had only driven Jeeps to that point, but being a daring young fellow of 21, I took the truck. I studied the instructions on the gearshift handle for shifting from one gear to another and off we went in a driving rainstorm. When we arrived at the Bayreuth theatre we were told that the theatre was filled and there was no room for us. We were about to leave, downhearted, when a man came to us and asked me what was the problem. When I told him that we could not get in to see the show, he told me to wait for him to return. He came back in a few minutes and told half of us to go with another person and the other half of us to go with him.

Needless to say, I followed him. He took us backstage to the wings. He turned out to be Larry Adler, the famous Harmonica Virtuoso. Backstage were Ingrid Bergman, Martha Tilton, a singer with the Big Bands of the Era and Jack Benny, himself. Ingrid Bergman, Martha Tilton and Larry Adler were just as nice as they could be and spoke to all of us at length. Jack Benny would have nothing to do with us and paced back and forth smoking his cigar. When he was called to appear on stage, he ground his cigar into the ground, straightened his jacket and went on stage. When Irgrid Bergmann was called, she said "Sergeant, hold my coat for me" and handed me her mink coat. I treasured that moment. She was gorgeous and gracious. She and Martha Tilton signed autographs for us, which I still have to this date.

The three years spent in service never leave you and although it is more than 65 years since I left the Army the memories of the events we endured and the lasting friendships I made are with me continually.

Our battalion, which stared out with 604 men is now down to a fraction of that number. Up until last year, we had reunions annually around the country.

When I went back to civilian life, I returned to City College. With the GI Bill of Rights I could have gone to almost any university but I did not want to leave my mother again. She had suffered enough when she found out her entire family had been destroyed in the holocaust.

With the credits I received from having attended Penn State, I was able to finish my education at City College by taking all the accounting and tax courses and graduating in June 1947.Therefore I was able to graduate in 2 ½ years. I went back to school evenings to take some courses I had missed such as an insurance course.

Now On To Enter The World Of Finance

I began to look for work during a very trying period when accounting jobs were difficult to find. My very "best friend" Leonard Fialkow had been a 4F and did not have to serve in the army. He had rheumatic fever as a child and it affected his heart. We were both in the class of 1945 but the college accelerated the program because of the war and my friend graduated in 1944. He got a job at Eisner and Lubin, CPAs. I asked Lenny if I could go to his firm looking for a job and use his name. He said I could go there but not to use his name. So much for a lifelong friendship.

Another friend of ours from high school and City College was Leonard Davis. He too was classified 4F and did not serve. He worked at Eisner and Lubin as well. He left there after a few years and moved to Poughkeepsie. He went into the insurance business and with family connections sold health insurance to a couple of utility companies. Leonard Davis had a heavily pocked mark face and looked much older that he really was. He apparently was able to present himself as a very mature individual. He came up with the idea of insurance for retired teachers and formed the Association for Retired Teachers. He did so well with that idea that the AARP (American Association for Retired Persons) was born. I suspect he went on to make billions. Leonard Fialkow was apparently not partnership material, even though he had been with Eisner and Lubin for many years. At that point in time, accounting firms were making partners from employees, He left Eisner and Lubin to join Davis. He was scheduled for a heart operation but he felt he had to make one more business trip before the operation. It turned out to be a fatal error on his part. He died at an early age.

By the summer of 1947 I had gotten engaged to Frances Seligsohn, my future wife. We were married December 14, 1947. I had met Frances while on a furlough in January 1944. It was fate that we should meet. I had a date with a girl from my high school class. Two of my buddies just happened to be on furlough at the same time. I cancelled my date and we three servicemen went to Manhattan to a USO dance. I spotted Frances at the dance. She was gorgeous. She allowed me to dance with her and gave me her address, although she would not let me take her home. We corresponded and started dating when I got out of service

We took a trip to Charleston, South Carolina to visit an army buddy Jack Kurtz. Jack had just begun his own business dealing in building supplies. I met his accountant while we were there. I told him I had just graduated and was looking for work in New York. He said that there was one accountant in New York that he had dealings with several years ago. He gave me his name, the name of the accounting firm and their address and permission to use his name. This is just after I met this man.

When I got back to New York I went to visit Wasserman and Taten CPAs at 501 Fifth Avenue. With my usual "chutzpa" aplomb, I told the receptionist to tell Mr. Harry Taten that Mr. Max Tannenbaum from Charleston, South Carolina was here to see him. Harry Taten came running out thinking that Max was there to see him. I told Mr. Taten the receptionist got it wrong and that I was sent by Mr. Tannenbaum to send his greetings. Mr. Taten invited me into his office and we talked for a few minutes about Max. He then called in Sam Gordon the manager and told him to put me to work. I suppose this incident supports the theory that it is not what you know but whom you know. Jack's accountant had done me a great service and I wrote to him thanking him for the introduction.

At that time an apprentice accountant needed three years of experience before being allowed to take the final part of the CPA exam. I was with Wasserman and Taten for almost three years and at that time it was unheard of for employees to be made partners. That came years later. I had already taken the first three parts of the examination. My sister had called to tell me that my marks had arrived and that I had passed three of the four parts. I told her I only took the three parts that she said I had passed. I took the final part of the CPA in November 1950, passed the first time I took the exam and became a CPA. The men were in the staff room discussing the exam when Mr. Wasserman came in. He had heard I was the only one in the firm who had passed the exam and asked me if I thought it would make me a better accountant. My reply was that my wife and my mother were very proud of me.

Mr. Taten's brother in law was an executive with a factoring company who referred many clients to them. Factoring at that time was very popular and consisted of the clients selling their accounts receivable without recourse to the factor. The business owner had to get permission from the factor to ship merchandise to a customer in order for the factor to advance funds and assume the risk of collecting the accounts receivable. I once heard Jack Wasserman tell one of the factoring companies to stop giving credit to one of his clients because of their financial position. Even though the clients were paying their fees, their loyalties were to the factors. We performed certified audits every six months for almost all of the clients and the resulting financial reports were submitted to the banks and factoring companies in addition to the clients, who had paid for the accounting.

Wasserman and Taten were a great training ground. I remember when taking the auditing part of the CPA exam, all I had to do was to think of the way we did things on the job. Harry Taten had a saying that he used time and time again. If one of the men went in to his office to review their work papers with him and Mr. Taten asked him how he arrived at a particular point and if the accountant replied that the bookkeeper had told him about it, Taten would scream, "Do not audit the bookkeeper, audit the books".

Harry Taten had another expression that he used and it was that his employees were not to defecate where they eat. Meaning of course no socializing with the clients' employees. But he violated his own directive by divorcing his wife and marrying the head secretary in his office.

Mr. Taten's son came to work for the firm and he became my junior assistant. We got along well and I did what I could to further his career.

The experience I received working for Wasserman and Taten served me well in all my years of practice. I definitely owe my passing the first time of the auditing examination to the schooling I received there. I distinctly remember calling on what I learned in answering the auditing questions. I had an experience while taking the practical accounting exam that I never had previously or since. I looked at this one problem and my mind went completely blank and all I saw was white. Lucky for me, another employee of Wasserman and Taten was sitting about ten feet from me and his test booklet was open to the same exam question.

Alvin was not the brightest guy in the world and I quickly figured that if Alvin was writing, I could get started and I did.

The majority of the clients were in the menswear field. Necktie piece good weavers, converters and manufacturers made up a good portion of the clientele. Every time we supervised the taking of the inventories I would come home with a bundle of neckties for friends, relatives and myself. It was many years after I stopped working there that I had to purchase a necktie.

One of their clients Jeff Greenhut conned the city of Scranton, Pennsylvania into building a factory building for him with the promise that he would put many local people to work. He was to pay rent for a dozen years and then the building would be his. With the modern weaving machinery and jacquard looms that he installed, he ended up employing just a hand full of people.

I handled that account and Mr. Greenhut and I became quite close. I would stay evenings with him to go over the production figures and then we had dinner at Manny Wolf, a great restaurant no longer in business. He suggested that I not place on my time records the evenings we spent together. He gave me great year-end gifts. He was very wealthy and successful. I met him socially at a wedding, years after I had gone in business for myself. He asked me why he had not heard from me. I told him that if I contacted him it would look like I was soliciting his business and he was too ostentatious to engage a small accounting firm. He did not deny it.

Every time I went to visit a new client, whether it was my bosses' client or my own, I always wanted to learn what was going on outside the office. I loved to learn how products were manufactured, assembled or created.

Manufacturing men's ties is an interesting process. In the trade, ties are called four-in-hand in deference to bow ties. The ties are sewed inside out and are then turned when they are completed. Ties are made in two sections. If you will look at your necktie, you will see where the narrow section is sewn onto the broad section. The piece of cloth under the ends of the ties is called tipping and the stiffening fabric inside the tie is call hymo. The pressing of the finished tie is done with a form placed inside the tie so that the finished products have a nice rolled edge instead of a flat appearance.

The buyer for the tie manufacturer purchases the tie fabrics. He will work with the sales person from the fabric converter. Tie fabrics are usually created in four or six color combinations. Once the buyer selects the design, he and the sales person will select color combinations to create the fabrics selected. If the order placed is large enough, the pattern selected will be confined to that customer and not sold to any other customer.

The fabric converter purchases the blank goods called greige goods, which are then dyed and usually screen-printed to order. Yarn dyed fabrics are treated with a starch to give them "body". If the pattern is woven into the fabric it probably means that it was woven on a jacquard loom.

My Bookkeeping Experience

Lands Me A Furrier Client.

When I first started working I told Sam the office manager that I had studied bookkeeping and that I had done some bookkeeping for my cousin's business. They sent me to a furrier on Fridays to do their bookkeeping and prepare the payroll. It was a famous furrier. If you have seen the motion picture Butterfield Eight, starring Elizabeth Taylor, you will remember there was a mink coat in the picture with the label in evidence reading "Reiss and Fabrizio". That was my furrier.

It was a fun place to work at because you never knew which celebrity was going to show up for a fur piece. Clark Gable came up for a fur lined cloth coat. Salvatore Dali came with his wife for a mink coat. Mr.Aaron Reiss was the salesman and Mr. Joseph Fabrizio the designer. Mr. Reiss quoted Mr. Dali $4,000 for the mink coat. Mr. Dali said he would paint a picture for them that would be worth $4,000. Mr. Reiss was no fool and he agreed. Mr. Dali took a canvas about 3 feet by 5 feet. Drew a horizontal line across the middle of the canvas. Painted the top half sky blue without a cloud and the bottom half sand color. He painted two small animals peeking out from behind two rocks and signed the painting DALI. Mr. Reiss had the painting appraised and of course it was worth the $4,000. I had always promised myself that someday I would purchase my wife a mink coat from Reiss and

Fabrizio. Years later, I did make an appointment for my wife and I and we were greeted with open arms. I looked around the showroom and the painting was nowhere in sight. I asked Aaron Reiss what happened to the DALI. He frowned and said he got an offer he could not refuse. He received $35,000 and spent it on fur skins, which he regretted. Shortly after that Mr. Dali died and of the course the painting only increased in value.

They had a genuine Italian countess working surreptitiously for them. She had access to their entire wardrobe and would wear one of their garments to all sorts of social functions and would attempt to steer customers to them, for which she was rewarded. The one celebrity I missed because she came on a day that I was not there was Paulette Goddard. She was a movie actress, quite beautiful and I believe had been married to Charlie Chaplin. In order to make a mink coat; Mr. Fabrizio would first sew a canvas garment from which the fur garment was constructed. I was told that Ms. Goddard was wearing a heavy wool suit and Mr. Fabrizio asked her to remove the jacket so he could measure her accurately. Word was that she had nothing under the jacket.

Once while working there, Mr. Reiss received a letter from Spain requesting a quotation for an ermine coat. He selected a bundle of ermine skins; an airline ticket to Spain and off he went to make the $10,000 sale.

A very funny incident happened with Reiss and Fabrizio. The sales tax department came to them to audit their books to ascertain if they had complied with their New York Sales Tax regulations. During their review they encountered sales invoice to Macy's department store for fur coats sold to them for resale with of course no sales tax consequences. The sales tax auditor communicated with Macy's store and requested a copy of their records detailing the purchases made from our client. The reply came with a notation with something to the effect, "we have no record of purchasing any items from the company under review," Sam Gordon handled all tax exams and he was floored. Needless to say, there were additional taxes, penalties and interest to be paid.

The first Christmas Reiss and Fabrizio gave me a gift of $250. At the company Christmas party I had received a bonus of $50. Mr. Wasserman asked if any clients had given me anything and when I told him about the $250, his quote was "those cheap bastards."

The manager, Sam Gordon, was the one who made the assignments for all of the employees. He sent me to a company that was listed on the American Stock Exchange. I will not name the company, but it manufactured razor blades and razors. The machinery that produced the products was fascinating. In reviewing the records I ascertained that the company was on the verge of bankruptcy. I discussed my findings with Sam and he said that one of W&T clients wanted to buy the company just for their listing on the American Stock Exchange. I asked Sam if we should buy any of the stock, which was selling for about $1 per share. Of course he told me that we are not permitted to buy any. However, if I bought any, then I should buy some shares for him. I did not buy any in my own name, but had my friend, Jack Kurtz buy some for Sam Gordon, himself and me. The stock doubled or tripled and then Sam called me and told me to immediately sell his stock because their client had backed out of the deal. I suggested to Sam that we hold on anyway because another buyer will probably come along. He said, "Do what you want but sell my stock." I called Jack, discussed the situation with him and we decided to hold on a while but to sell Sam's stock. I was right because another company did buy the company and the stock rose again. We sold shortly thereafter and did well. It was the only illegal thing that I ever did during my accounting career. I guess I am in the same company with Martha Stewart.

The job entailed some travel. I went to Indianapolis with another accountant. We stayed at the Claypool Hotel, known as the Cesspool. We audited a tie manufacturer there and then went on to St. Louis for another tie manufacturer.

The longest out of town trips took me to Mt. Gilead North Carolina. We spent a couple of weeks there and sometimes we were allowed to come home weekends. It was a woman's underwear factory owned by a Moses Richter. He owned peach orchids as well. He liked to play Gin Rummy and we had instructions to humor him and play with him. All my losses went on my expense report.

One night, just before going to bed, I went to the local diner for a glass of milk and a piece of apple pie. I asked the waitress to place a piece of cheese on the pie and warm it in the oven. She did what I asked and served it to me. When I was through eating, I asked the waitress what I owed her. She said "a quarter, ten cents for the milk and fifteen cents for the pie." Remember this was in the late 1940s. I said what about the cheese and she replied that if I was crazy enough to eat it, then there was no charge.

I started looking for a better paying job and was answering newspaper ads. One day Mr. Taten called me into his office, sat me down, and asked me why I was looking for another job. I asked him if he would tell me how he knew, I would tell him why. He said I had answered their ad. I figured I was about to be fired, so I told him of all the things I thought was wrong with the firm and that I needed more money. He asked if I would stay if I received a raise. I told him what I needed and he said that would put me pay wise ahead of someone who was there longer than I, but my Christmas bonus would make up for it.

So, believing him to be a man of his word—I stayed.

Came Christmas, I was expecting a bonus of at least $500. The amount I received was the same as I received the previous year. So, when Sam Gordon went to talk to the two bosses about the raises we would receive for the coming year, I told him not to bother discussing any raise for me as I was leaving. Immediately I was called into to talk to Wasserman and Taten. I told them what I had expected in the form a bonus based on the agreement I had with Mr. Taten. Instead of them admitting their shortcoming, Mr. Wasserman started berating Mr. Taten for making such a rash promise, telling him he had no right to make such a promise.

I told them that it was time for me to start my own accounting practice and that my wife stood with me with the decision. They kept me for over two hours trying to talk me out of the idea and telling me of all the trials and tribulations I would encounter. I told them that they had done it and apparently they did not regret it. They said that they knew that I did not have enough clients to begin with and they wanted me to stay on and work for them on a per diem basis. That suited me just fine, since I would need the money. Obviously they deemed me to be a valuable employee and did not want to lose me. However, in 1950 employees were not made partners. No promise was made to me that if I stayed eventually I would be made a partner.

Fortunately for me, I did not stay with W&T. Many years later they merged into another accounting firm. That firm ended up in bankruptcy and all the partners lost their entire pensions. If I had remained with W&T, I more than likely would have made partner and regretted it.

I think that young people becoming accountants today do not think in terms of starting their own practice after they pass the CPA exam. They think in terms of possibly becoming a partner where they are working or getting a decent job with one of the clients they service. It is a different world.

Now I Am On My Own.

I started out with one day a week on my own and four days per diem. Then two for me and three for them and so on until I did not need them any longer. I never made any attempt to usurp any of their clients. However, people who had worked for their clients and who went into business for themselves would call upon me to be their accountant. Harry Taten kept asking me if I was finished fooling around and was I ready to come back to work for them? I told him everything was working out well and that I was happy being my own boss.

During those days three men would get together, a salesman, a designer and a cutter. They would raise about $30,000 between them, rent a showroom and cutting room and go into business making ladies clothing. Some succeeded and some failed.

Donald Jacobs, worked for Jeff Greenhut keeping the production records, left his job and went into business with his wife. They had a very dear friend of theirs design a line of table place mats. They hired me as their accountant. Unfortunately, they used most of the funds that they had in renovating a very ornate showroom and ran out of funds before they really ever got started. Their very dear friend turned out to be none other than Andy Warhol. Years after they were no longer in business they slowly had to sell the original sketches. I think by the time Andy Warhol died they had already sold all the sketches. Mrs. Jacobs used to model her hands and had them insured for a great deal of money.

Finally I stopped working for Wasserman and Taten. But, I still needed some per diem work from time to time. I did some work for a brother in law of Seymour Schwarz, another buddy from the army. He worked on the philosophy that since he could not make enough of a living from the regular monthly fees, he would tell his clients when they had IRS examinations that he had to bribe the agent. He would give some money to the agents but kept the lion's share for himself. He tried to make certain that his clients had their tax returns examined. Our relationship was very short lived.

One of Wasserman and Taten's substantial clients had always treated me well and liked the work I did for him. Nat Sheinman owned many corporations and used several accounting firms. His personal secretary was Dorothy Hughes and she and I always got along. He took over a dress factory in Poughkeepsie, New York and discussed with Ms Hughes which accounting firm he should use. She suggested that he give this client to me. He agreed and told her to get in touch with me.

She called Wasserman and Taten and spoke to the office manager Evelyn Posner. She asked if they had my home telephone or address. Evelyn immediately put Mr. Taten on the phone. He wanted to know why she needed me and she told him it was a personal matter. Evelyn knew exactly where to contact me and had my home address and phone number but instead she then gave Ms. Hughes the last place where I had done some per diem work. Ms. Hughes called them and they gave her my home phone number. She called my home and spoke to my wife. Frances gave her my answering service. She called that number and they told her where to find me. Thank goodness she was determined to find me and made five calls. She called me and put her boss on the phone. He was short and direct. "Eddie meet me 6 o'clock tomorrow morning at my apartment on Central Park West." Needless to say I was there a 6 AM and so began a relationship lasting many years.

He owned corporations that created a complete vertical setup. He bought the bales of cotton, had a mill that made the yarn, had weaving plants that made the cloth and sewing plants that made the ladies garments. He sold the garments to the finest stores in the country and had his own retail outlet shops. He made and lost fortunes and at one time owed the banks so much money that they could not afford to allow him to fail and he always bounced back and made another fortune. He was a substantial contributor to the fledgling State of Israel.

I always considered Evelyn Posner a friend of mine and really was annoyed that she just did not give my home phone number to Ms. Hughes. One morning, while I was still working there full time, Evelyn told me that she would like to take me to lunch and discuss something with me. Suited me fine. At that time social security has just been extended to self-employed persons. Up to that point only employees had been covered. Evelyn told me that her father was a barber all his working life and had never filed a tax return. She asked me what he could do now to try to get social security when he turns 65. I told her to have her father immediately start filing tax returns and there is an excellent possibility he will not get caught for not filing tax returns for all the years he should have been paying taxes. I am sure she and her father followed my advice but it did not carry any weight when it came to doing me a good turn.

Nat Sheinman owned two dress factories in Saugerties and Poughkeepsie. I drove to Saugerties every Friday checked the production and payroll records and signed the payroll checks. Then drove down to Poughkeepsie to do the same thing there. I did it in all kinds of weather for several years. Once while driving on the thruway towards Saugerties I broke a fan belt and the car started to overheat. A state trooper came along and asked if he could help. I told him what I thought the problem was. He said he would go buy a fan belt and come back and put it on for me. I told him that he would get filthy and that is was very nice of him but it was a bad idea. He drove off to find a gas station and said he would be back. He returned in about ten minutes and told me that the mechanic at the gas station said that my car was probably cooled off enough to drive safely the half-mile to the gas station. The state trooper stopped all traffic and I followed him to the gas station and my car was repaired. I asked the trooper for his name and address so that I could send him some ties. I told him I was on my way to a dress factory and I could send his wife a dress. He said he was not married but had a girlfriend. I asked for her address and he said "same as mine."

The man who ran the shop in Poughkeepsie was Max Stagg. Max had previously owned the shop, but through gambling had lost a great deal of money and turned it over to Mr. Sheinman, with the proviso that he remain on to manage the shop. Max's wife was killed in an auto accident. She was the passenger in the front seat of the car. Her daughter in law was sitting behind her. Max was driving and had a head on collision. At that time, the backs of the front seats did not lock into place and there were no seal belts. His daughter in law came forward with such force, that she crushed the chest of his wife.

Harry Weinstein and his wife ran the Saugerties shop. Lovely, hard working people. They lived in Kingston and occasionally I would have dinner with them and spend the night at their home and then go on to Poughkeepsie the next day. During the summer months I would take my family with me and they would enjoy a day in the country.

One of the stores to whom Nat Sheinman sold garments was located in Naples, Florida. They owed in excess of $50,000 and were late with their payments. My client told them that he was sending me down to review their books. The storeowner was very hostile when I arrived on the scene. The name of the store was the Bamboo Shop. It was located on the waterfront. Customers could come off their boats and shop. The owner would ply the husbands with drinks while the women shopped. His presentation of his merchandise was magnificent. All the merchandise was color coordinated and he had merchandise from top American and European manufacturers. His books revealed that he was overstocked with inventory but given time he could work out of his dilemma. I had taken my Polaroid camera with me and took pictures of the exterior and interior of the store. Over and above the store in Naples he rented another store in New England during the summer. He and his wife would pack up the entire inventory and drive two Cadillacs with trailers from Florida to New England. I told my client to set up a series of note payments for the next year and liquidate the debt in that fashion. On my advice my client continued to sell him and I went back the next year to check on the progress. This time the hostility was less but still not entirely friendly. Eventually all worked out and surprisingly the next spring I got a call from Naples wanting to know if I would become his accountant. I told him I would be pleased to be his accountant but I would have to talk to my client first. My client told me to go right ahead and work with him.

One of the companies owned by this same client was a cotton mill in Hamilton, Rhode Island. This company was a client of my old boss and I handled the account while I was still working there. It was a fascinating business. The client had purchased the textile mill and the real estate from an old staunch New Englander whose family had owned the business for generations. He had no descendants and sold the business. The plant had been in existence since the early 1800s. It was located on the waterfront. Ships came up from the south with bales of cotton. The cotton was spun into yarn and then woven into narrow webbing for mattress and parachutes straps among other uses. The accounting books were in storage dating back more than a hundred years. They were written in a magnificent Spenserian handwriting. The bookkeeper was probably in his 80s and had been with the company all his life. He showed me these old fascinating books of account.

I would have loved to acquire one of the books for my own collection.

He reminded me of the bookkeeper who worked all his life for this one company. Every morning he came into his office. He took this key out of his pocket, inserted it into the middle drawer in his huge desk. He opened the drawer part way, looked down into the drawer, shoved the drawer closed and relocked it. He finally passed away and after the funeral the entire office staff found the key and rushed to the office. They opened the drawer with great anticipation. They all looked into the drawer and saw to their amazement an aged browned small piece of paper glued to the bottom of the drawer. And written on the paper, barely legible were the words "the debit is the side towards the window."

Over and above the mill that was purchased, the client acquired a mill town consisting of about twenty-five one, two and three room homes. The homes had no indoor plumbing, no central heating and an outside toilet. The rents collected from the tenant employees were minimal. Nat Sheinman had a partner, Marty Nelson, for this project. Marty and Nat had no desire to be landlords. Marty called together the entire tenant employees and offered to sell the small houses for $1,500 and the larger ones for $2,500. Immediately all the tenants purchased their homes for cash. I went to this plant quarterly. On the next visit I was amazed to see that these people who had lived all their lives under appalling conditions when they were tenants, now that they were owners immediately installed indoor plumbing, central heating and in some cases central air conditioning. Obviously they were not prepared to improve the landlord's property no matter how they themselves survived.

Another investment made by Nat was to purchase an upscale ladies retail shop in Chestnut Hill, Pennsylvania, which is a suburb of Philadelphia. Nat asked me to handle the accounting. A lovely aged lady ran the shop by the name of Mary Hart. In the summer time she would rent a store on Shelter Island Heights, New York. She would attempt to sell all the merchandise he would send to her plus what she purchased from other manufacturers. My family became very friendly with Mrs.

Hart and her daughter Donna. When she came to New York on a buying trip, my wife would join her for the day. She would bring her records to my office in Great Neck. When my oldest Susan daughter went off to Brandeis University, Mary took her on a shopping excursion and outfitted her from top to bottom.

At the beginning of my accounting practice I would sometimes have to see three clients in one day just to earn $50. It was usually diners, gas stations and bars and grills. One of the diners was in Verona, New Jersey. I worked on the books in the home of the owner since there was no decent place to work in the diner. The wife was a handsome, prim WASP. I would not dream of saying anything off color while I was there. One morning while I was at work, we were both listening to Arthur Godfrey on the radio. The wife turned to me and said; "he is only man other than my husband who I would allow to put his shoes under my bed." I was shocked.

While struggling to make a living and expand my practice as I was now a father and my wife was no longer working, I did whatever I could to acquire new clients. I saw Cousin Benny at a family function and he asked me how I was doing. I told him of my struggle and he suggested that I give up my private practice and go to work for the Internal Revenue Service. He said the job was 9 to 5, five days a week, vacations, health insurance and a pension. During the 1950s the IRS was strife with agents who would take bribes to reduce tax assessments. The term of the day was "T and E and out by three." T and E meaning Travel and Entertainment. Those were the expense items on the tax returns that were usually overstated and subject to disallowances. I told Benny that with bribes continually offered to me, I might very well accept them and then I would not sleep at night. His answer was one I will never forget. He said, "If you cannot sleep nights forget about it." So, I stayed in public accounting.

Things Begin To Look Up

Cousin Benny was investigated several times by the IRS, but they never did anything to him. He was able to establish substantial side income from owning a part of his brother's business. His wife had several near nervous breakdowns.

I got a call from Cousin Benny one day and he said that he knows an accountant who needed help and I should call him and arrange to meet with him. I called Max Steiner. Max had an office on 44th street between 5th and 6th avenue. His entire practice consisted of large over the road trucking companies. He had two employees and a secretary and did no accounting himself. He knew all the intricacies of the Interstate Commerce Commission and knew how to obtain financing for his clients. He wanted me to run the accounting practice. It sounded interesting and we began a relationship.

At that point the interstate trucking business was completely regulated by the ICC. Every trucking company had what was called its "Authority". This meant that each trucking company had the right to travel specified amounts of miles on specified roads to service their clients. The trucking companies that had been in business before the creation of the ICC were granted grandfather rights. To expand their territories they either had to purchase a competitor or apply to the ICC for the right to increase their territory and follow their customers as they moved elsewhere. Their competitors would enter their objections to the ICC and a decision would be rendered. These Authorities were worth millions of dollars, but became absolutely worthless the moment deregulation came into being during the Reagan administration. You did not have to be an attorney to represent your client. Those who practiced were called ICC practitioners.

Max had as clients Amsterdam Dispatch based in Amsterdam New York. Long Island Delivery Company located in Nassau County New York, two milk carriers McBride Trucking and Van Rompaye Palmer based in Goshen and Chester New York. In addition he had two Virginia clients Novick Transfer Company and Allegheny Freight Lines both based in Winchester, Virginia. I took control of the auditing with the staff of two and Max just smoked his cigars. He would do the driving to Virginia and sit around and chew the fat with the clients while we worked. There were other small trucking companies with specific problems from time to time. I retained my own clients and continued to service them until I would determine how this new arrangement would work out.

It was interesting and enjoyable work with nice intelligent people to work with. The ICC required an annual report that made a corporate tax return look like child's play. Max knew how to charge fees and did well for himself. The two trucking companies in Virginia were particularly enjoyable to work with. Novick Trucking was owned by Abraham Jerome Novick a/k/a AJ Novick. He came to the United States as a youngster and became a peddler, as did many immigrants. How he ended up in Winchester I never found out. He bought a truck and began carrying his wares and others from Winchester to New York. He created his business before the creation of the ICC and so his ICC authority was grandfathered to him. His business grew to the point where his fleet consisted of hundreds of trucks, tractors and semi-trailers. He had two sons Marshall and Robert and they both were in the business. The controller with whom I dealt regularly was Charles Anderson. A lovely man but not the greatest accountant. I tread on thin ice to point out the errors of his ways. I never admonished him and gently suggested the changes that should be made. He never commented on my corrections but just went ahead and changed his entries. We became fast friends. He lived in Berryville, about ten miles from Winchester and owned a Black Angus farm. I would spend my evenings with him and occasionally he would butcher a cow and we would have Black Angus steaks for dinner. Charles died an unfortunate and untimely death. He went into the local hospital for a simple gall bladder operation and died of gaseous gangrene.

Three gentlemen owned Allegheny Freight Lines. Maurice Grove who lived on a two hundred-year-old family owned farm in Luray, Virginia. Forrest Sirbaugh who lived in Winchester. He and Maurice had formed the company and subsequently allowed Jack McAboy, who also lived in Winchester to buy his one-third interest. Winchester Virginia is the home of Patsy Cline and lives in the glory of her memory. Jack ran the company. Maurice dropped in occasionally. Forrest came in every day and in his youth had been a good salesman, but now he just sat around and collected his paycheck.

Maurice was a devout born again Christian. He knew when I was coming down and he would leave literature for me to read. If I got into a religious conversation with him, I would ask him "if Jesus Christ came back tomorrow, would he go to my synagogue or to your church?" He was not close-minded and agreed with me about my question. He ran a Hereford cattle farm. One time he invited me to come down to the farm and spend a night with them. I was happy to accept his invitation and had a lovely home cooked meal and then was shown to my bedroom. It consisted of an iron bed with a thin mattress, a small dresser and a bare bulb hanging on an electric string from the ceiling.

Many times when I would be in Winchester, some of the men who worked at Allegheny and Novick would get together in the evening for a poker game. I am far from a great poker player, but for some uncanny reason I usually ended up a winner at the end of the night. Marshall Novick could drink six beers during the game and never had the need to get up to relieve himself.

I began to install an IBM computer system for Allegheny Freight Lines, Inc. For those of you old enough to remember, we were installing a Series 50 system. That meant that every component part of the system would work at 50 units per minute. The punch card machine, the verifiers, the printers, the sorters and everything else operated at a speed that we would laugh at today with what has happened to computers since then. Jack and I were invited to go to IBM school upstate New York for a week. We both went and met with accountants, controllers, owners and bookkeepers from other trucking companies. We were treated royally and had a most enjoyable week. Allegheny's business was more unusual than most other trucking companies. They operated in the states of Virginia, West Virginia, Maryland and Pennsylvania and had about six terminals located in these states. Rarely did they pick up freight at a customer and deliver it to the ultimate recipient. They received freight from other trucking companies, moved the freight along their territory and then usually gave it to another trucking for the ultimate delivery. This made for a complicated bookkeeping system but one that they mastered and made substantial annual profits. It meant that if they were picking up freight that was prepaid, they billed their customer. If they turned over the freight to another carrier, they would be billed for the other carrier's portion of the revenue. If the freight they picked up were shipped on a collect basis, then they would bill the carrier to whom they gave the freight for ultimate delivery for their portion of the revenue. Sometimes they were sandwiched in between a carrier who gave them freight; they moved it along their territory and then gave it to another carrier for ultimate delivery. So you can envision the complicated billing situation especially since they were producing 1200 to 1400 pros (invoices) a day.

I wrote and delivered a paper describing in detail Allegheny's operation and the use of the IBM systems. I received a call from IBM asking me if they could use my paper for an advertising brochure to sell their system. I asked them how much would I be paid. No payment was in the offing but they did offer me a job, which I turned down.

After about two years I told Max Steiner that I must either become a partner or I would have to leave. He was not interested in a partnership and so I left. I did not notify any of his clients that I was leaving, nor did I solicit their work. A few weeks after we parted company, and obviously he had to tell his clients that I had departed, I got a call from Jack McAboy. He said "you son of a bitch you left us high and dry with the IBM installation incomplete." I apologized and explained that I could not work for Max any longer. He asked me to come down, complete the installation and become their accountant since they had not seen Max do anything for them in years. They were financially stable and did not need Max to obtain bank loans for them. I told Jack to speak to Max and work it out with him. Max knew nothing about computers and had no choice but to agree to give up the client. I worked for Allegheny for years until Maurice and Forrest died and Jack sold out.

About a year after I began working as their accountant, Allegheny's main terminal and office in Winchester burned to the ground. I was not present during the time of the fire but I saw pictures that were taken of the fire. Of course the three owners were immediately called and told of the fire. Jack McAboy dressed and rushed over to the terminal. Forrest, so he told me later, was just so upset that he put on a shirt and his shoes and was heading out the front door, when he wife told him the he had better put on a pair of pants.

At the risk of life and limb some of the men threw a chain around the huge safe that sat in the office. They attached the chain to a tractor and pulled the safe out of the office. After it had cooled off sufficiently for them to open they safe, they found in the safe a bottle of aspirins and nothing else. All the records had been burned to a crisp. However, since they had five other terminals, they were able with much effort to piece together the accounts receivable. Each of the other terminals produced their own invoices and kept a record of each invoice. So it was only the invoices that were produced in Winchester that were destroyed in the fire.

What was amazing is that the customers, who of course were aware of the fire and could, have tried not to pay their bills, almost without exception mailed in their checks for what they owed. Temporary offices were rented in town and they got back to work. The terminal and office were rebuilt rather quickly and they were able to move back to their facilities within a few months.

Maurice Grove went with his church group, which he personally financed, to the Holy Land. Being at heart a farmer, he spent time in the Holy Land looking at the progress the Israelites had made in the desert, the irrigation systems and the farming. His comment to me when he returned was that "those Jews have done some great job on the farms".

Now It Gets Real Interesting

Maurice, better known as JM Grove, came down with cancer and was dying. His wife, son and daughter were attending services one Sunday at their small country church. The minister of the church was financed by JM. This Sunday there was a visiting minister from Jerry Falwell's organization. He was preaching about estate planning and how if the parishioners would leave their money to Jerry Falwell's Liberty Baptist College, he would do the Lord's work and there would be absolutely no estate taxes. Mrs. Grove asked the visiting minister to come to see her husband knowing he might be interested in talking to him. The minister came to the house and spoke to JM. He asked if JM had adequately provided for his wife and children and was told that they were. The minister then told JM if he left all his estate to the Jerry Falwell organization, they would pay Mrs. Grove 8% income from the funds he would donate for the rest of her life and that Uncle Sam and the Commonwealth of Virginia would not get one penny in taxes. That is just what JM wanted to hear. He had been obsessed with having to pay estate taxes upon his demise. There was a tape of this conversation. At first I thought the minister was the one who taped it for his protection, but it turned out that Mrs. Grove was the taping freak and she played it for me.

The next morning the minister returned with a crew of people from Jerry Falwell's organization. Attorneys, ministers and office people. They had already prepared a new will for JM, which he signed leaving his entire interest in Allegheny Freight Lines to Jerry Falwell's Liberty College. JM Grove died shortly after he signed the will.

Jack McAboy received a call asking for a meeting so that the funds could be turned over to Jerry Falwell's Liberty College. Jack called me and asked me to come down and prepare a financial statement as of the date of death of JM Grove. I prepared the Balance Sheet and Profit and Loss Statement and stayed for the meeting. The meeting was held at the home of Forrest Sirbaugh. All the dignitaries from the Falwell organization came to the meeting with the exception of Mr. Falwell himself. I distributed copies of the financial report to all present and then explained that the one-third interest owned by JM Grove was about $2,000,000. The financial officer from the Falwell organization then went into a lengthy speech telling of his appreciation of the funds they were about to receive, but based on his interpretation of the financial report and the profits that were made by Allegheny Freight Lines, the Falwell group was entitled to substantially more money than was being offered. He said the goodwill of the company was not considered in my offer and that he must insist that the offer be increased to recognize the goodwill of the company.

I anticipated his tirade and brought forth the stockholders' agreement. The three stockholders had agreed many years prior to that date that no goodwill is to be considered in liquidating any of the stockholders shares, by a desire to sell to the remaining stockholders or by death. So, the Falwell group went home with a measly $2,000,000.

Now the estate tax returns, federal and Virginia had to be prepared and filed. Mrs. Iva Grove engaged a local attorney in Luray and we began communicating by phone. He did not know if I was a follower of Falwell and I certainly did not know of his beliefs. We both felt like we were walking on eggshells. Ultimately we both realized that neither of us had any love for Falwell. We worked together preparing the estate tax returns. If Mr. Grove had left the $2,000,000 to the Falwell organization with no strings attached, then the entire amount would have been deemed a charitable contribution and entirely deductible. However, since Mrs. Grove was to receive 8% income for the rest of her live, the charitable contribution was diminished by an amount, which ultimately required the estate to pay taxes of $300,000. Mrs. Grove became incensed. She told me that they promised JM on his deathbed that there would be no taxes and she had it on her tape. I told her that I was certain that she would not have to pay the $300,000 personally and that Falwell's Liberty College would be glad to pay the tax. That did not satisfy her one bit and she directed the attorney to get back her $2,000,000. She would not be dissuaded. Reverend Falwell could not stand any adverse publicity to appear in any newspaper, radio or TV. So the $2,000,000 was returned to her. They told her that they had already used some of the funds for the building of a dormitory and they would give her a mortgage on the building and liquidate it in a short period of time. She took the money and immediately distributed the funds to her pet charities that consisted of other Born Again Christian Organizations. It was a lot of fun engaging in the negotiations and I told you accounting does not have to be boring.

I had not made any attempt to contact Charles Anderson or the Novicks on my visits to Winchester while serving Alleghany Freight Lines. This would have been about 1954. One day Charles called Jack McAboy and asked him to have me call him on my next trip to Winchester. I called him and he said that he understood my ethical position with reference to not contacting him or AJ. However, he thought that we were friends and he missed me. He had discussed with AJ his feelings about changing the accounting work to me. I did the same thing again and asked either AJ or Charles to work it out with Max Steiner. I began staying once again at Charles's home and enjoying his steaks and company.

And so I now had two substantial trucking companies as my clients. Max has been foolish in not allowing me to become his partner. He retired soon after that.

Since I now had these several substantial interstate trucking companies as clients, I decided to apply to join the Land Transport Committee of the New York State Society of Certified Public Accountants. I was accepted as a member and joined other CPAs who either worked for the largest trucking companies in this country as chief financial officers or controllers. In addition there were members like myself who were in public accounting and audited the large and medium sized trucking firms. The chairman of the committee was an accountant and attorney with the giant law firm Simpson Thatcher. We became friendly and when he stepped down as chairman, I became chairman of the committee. It was interesting to discuss with the other members of the committee the workings and problems of the trucking industry. Unfortunately, when the trucking industry became deregulated, that was the death knell for the Land Transport Committee and it no longer exists as a part of the New York State Society of CPAs.

In addition to joining the Land Transport Committee I became a member of the Metropolitan Society of Motor Carrier Accountants. This was a much larger group of people and all the members were also either working for large trucking companies or were like myself outside auditors. All the large trucking companies with headquarters in the metropolitan were represented in this organization. We met for dinner once a month at Rosoffs restaurant, which was located in the 40s just Off-Broadway. There was usually a guest speaker or some other function. One cold miserable raining night I attended the meeting. There were only fourteen of us attending. The speaker for the evening was with Remington Rand. At that time Remington Rand was producing primitive computers. At the end of his talk he raffled off a dozen Remington Rand electric razors. As I said we were only 14 so two of us would not go home with an electric razor. You guessed it, I did not win. The speaker said that if he knew that there would be only 14 men, he would have brought 14 electric razors but he could not accommodate me and the other loser.

I befriended two members of the organization. One was Herb Waxman who was a sole practitioner like me. We began discussing joining forces and he brought in a friend of his by the name of Harold Pepper. We did form a partnership know as Waxman, Pepper and Gotbetter, CPAS. We opened an office at 1776 Broadway, which was on the corner of Broadway and 57th Street. I was low man on the totem pole. I brought in less gross fees than Waxman or Pepper. We stayed together for a few years. Pepper said that if we did not move to Long Island he would have a heart attack. Coming to New York every day during the tax season was a strain. We all lived on Long Island and so we looked for an office in Great Neck. We found a suitable office in the heart of Great Neck.

Waxman held out bonuses he received from one or more of his trucking clients and I felt that I was being charged for a larger share of the office expenses than was appropriate. We parted company. Unfortunately, Harold Pepper came from a family of men with bad hearts. His father and a brother had both died in their forties from heart attacks. Harold had a heart attack and died while visiting his children at summer camp. We had already dissolved the partnership but Harold, I, and a couple of other accountants were sharing an office in Great Neck. Harold never should have been an accountant. All he wanted to do was to socialize and attempt to obtain clients. He did some shady things that we did not uncover until after his death and if he had lived it is possible that he would have gotten into a great deal of trouble with the law.

The other man who I befriended at the organization was Harold Rosegarten. He lived in Great Neck and was related to the owners of Yale Transport. Yale was a giant in the trucking industry in New York City. They had a huge sign facing the Westside highway, which was a profile of a tractor, and trailer advertising their name. They were basically consolidators, which meant that they would receive cartons from local manufacturers in New York City via trucking companies. These cartons were destined for large department stores all over the United States. They had computer conveyor belts that sorted the cartons by destination and then loaded the freight into their trailers for movement across the country.

We rented a room in our office to Harold Rosegarten. He did some work for Yale and had other clients. He introduced me to the owner of Yale and I ended up doing some cost accounting for them. It was interesting work and paid well.

MY DOG AND A CLIENT SAVE MY LIFE

I am living on borrowed time. My daughter Susan married Tom in our home in the Hamptons on a beautiful warm day in April 27 years ago.

The caterer arrived from Manhattan with all the food. She placed it on the floor of our kitchen. My dog, SAM, a black standard poodle went over to sniff the bags. The caterer screamed to get the dog away from the food. I reached behind SAM to pull him away. He was not aware that it was me and bit me on my right hand between the thumb and the forefinger. I bled profusely and Spencer, my other son-in-law rushed me to the Southhampton hospital with my hand wrapped in gauze.

The nurses at the emergency room immediately took care of me when we told them of the pending wedding ceremony. They immersed my hand in an antiseptic and a doctor stitched the wound. He told me to have a doctor remove the stitches in about a week. We returned to the wedding and all went well for the rest of the afternoon.

When I got back to my office, I called my client Dr. J. Wright Barry and told him what had happened and could he remove the stitches. He made an appointment for me and I then said that since I had not been to a doctor in at least five years, could he schedule a complete physical examination. He did and when I arrived at his office, he removed the stitches and gave me a complete examination. He said that there was something on the back of my left shoulder that should be looked at by a dermatologist.

I followed his advice and scheduled an appointment with Dr. Lillian Graf. She saw what he pointed out and removed a slice for biopsy. She told me that it pink in color and was nothing to concerned about. The biopsy proved to be a melanoma. She called me as soon as she had the result and I went to see her.

I was petrified and assumed that my life was over. Norman W. had recently died from a melanoma. Dr. Graf send me to a surgeon at New York Hospital. My wife and I went as soon as we could. The surgeon, seeing that I was in a state of panic, calmed me down by telling me that my melanoma was only .45 millimeters. He showed me a book which displayed the percentages of success in removing the melanoma and my chances were 95%. If the melanoma had been 4 millimeters or more the success rate was next to zero.

I asked the doctor what does he do when a patient comes in with a melanoma of 4 millimeters or more? He said "I do not show them the book".

When I was in the army I had a serious case of acne. After a field march my undershirt would be soaked in blood. I had to get up at 5 AM and go to the hospital for ultra violet ray treatments Which probably caused the melanoma. One of the doctors told me that I should not have been admitted to the army with my condition. I said "so let me out". He laughed and told me that would take care of it.

We Expand To A Partnership

Fred Weinstein was dating my niece Sari, my wife's sister's daughter, and was attending Brooklyn College studying accounting. He came to work for me part time and helped me with my growing practice. When he graduated I told him to get as many interviews as he could and see what was available in the accounting field and then come talk to me. Fred was a very bright young man and was offered a job with almost every firm that he visited. We sat down to discuss the offers he had received. He told me that the best offer he had been for $14,000 a year. I told him that I would pay him the same $14,000 and if he passed the CPA exam in three years that I would immediately make him a partner. I said go home and think about it. He said, "that there was nothing to think about, he would stay with me and did I think that he could make as much as $25,000 a year someday." Every so often I remind him of it.

Fred passed the CPA exams, as I did, the first time he took them and became my partner as I promised him with no investment on his part. We have been known as Gotbetter and Weinstein, CPAs for more than 30 years. We have no written partnership agreement and we never saw the need for it. It may seem a little strange to others not to have a written arrangement but we have worked together as a team and have rarely had the slightest disagreement

I did not know if I could afford to hire Fred full time, but at the same time, I could not afford to lose him as long as he was willing to stay with me. We did not have a great many clients but slowly our practice grew and grew. We never grew large enough to hire any employee full time. We had used per diem help over the years.

My daughter Amy graduated from the University of Pennsylvania and then went on to get her Masters from Dartmouth. She became an accountant and went to work at several jobs in public and private accounting and passed the CPA exam. She left her job and she started to raise a family.

When her two children were old enough to care for themselves she began to work for us part time. I turned over to her several clients and she would service them. Every one of the clients loved her. One of my clients needed someone like Amy to help her. When I suggested she let Amy come to work for her, the client said that was nepotism and was not interested. After a few weeks and having gone through several prospective assistants, she called me and told me to send Amy to see her. She engaged Amy and told me later that is was the best decision she had ever made. Amy charges a fee to these clients directly and we only got involved with the year-end work and tax returns.

Amy would help us tax season but this past tax season I made Amy an offer she could not refuse and she gave me a great deal of time. She checked almost every return I prepared and I checked those she prepared. In addition she found time to assist Fred. Fred also hired a per diem assistant for the tax season.

We have had our office in Great Neck, NY for many years and have occupied offices at several locations. In our last office, we were told to move by our landlord when our lease expired. We were occupying a part of the third floor and the other tenant told our landlord that either they obtain use of the entire floor or they will move. So out we went. We were looking for space when the real estate agent told us of another accountant who had just lost a partner and had space available. Fred and I were not happy about sharing space, but we went to look at the office. It was an ideal situation and the accountant seemed to be someone with whom we could co-exist.

It turned out to be a great move. Herbert Hirshhorn was both a CPA and an attorney. He was a kind, friendly and great individual. He did very little legal work other than an occasional will or estate. We got along just great.

He had as a secretary Mary McLennan who was with him for about 30 years. A bright lovely woman.

Unfortunately he became ill with cancer and passed away about a year and half ago. Fred negotiated to purchase his practice from his widow. It has kept Fred extremely busy but it also giving him the opportunity to vastly increase his personal income way beyond the $25,000 he hoped to earn one day.

Opportunities Come Along For Investments

I have remained friends with Jack Kurtz ever since we both got out of the army. We are almost like brothers. Unfortunately he still lives in Charleston and we do not get to see each other very often but we speak occasionally. We have gone into several joint ventures and have done reasonably well financially. His wife was Miss Charleston in the early 50s and was really beautiful. She is a lovely woman.

Jack had heard of the Concord Hotel in the Catskills and wanted to take a short vacation by going to the Concord Hotel. He called and told me to make reservations for the four of us. I told my wife what Jack wanted and she said to make reservations for him and Florence, his wife. She would not go because Jack would pick up the tab and it would embarrass her. Who am I to argue with the little woman? So, I called Jack and told him that I have made reservations for the two them and the reason why we cannot go. He said to tell Frances that he insists that we go along with them and that he would let us pay our own way. We went off to the Concord and had a lovely extended weekend vacation. If any of you have ever been to the Concord, then you know that Sunday morning you get on line at the cashier to pay your bill. Of course when it came my turn to pay my bill, I was told that it had already been paid. I confronted Jack and told him that he was about to get me into big trouble. His reply was that he paid both bills with a company check, for the business meeting that we all attended, and that he is giving me 10% of Charleston Plywood and Lumber Company. So I should stop fretting since I just paid for my share of the bill. This explanation satisfied my wife.

Jack bought a plywood distributor in Atlanta in the middle 1950s. I got my percentage of that company and for about two years I flew to Atlanta every Thursday to review the records and sign the payroll checks. I flew home on Fridays. Frances and I were seriously considering moving to Atlanta because it really is a lovely city. But, before we had to make our minds up, we sold the company. When Jack and I first started going to Atlanta, we used to check into a hotel. It was always a problem because of all the conventions held in Atlanta. We then rented a room in a residential hotel on Peachtree Street. If you remember Bert Parks, the TV master of ceremonies, then you will appreciate that we used to see him almost every week while he was visiting his mother in our residential hotel.

AJ Novick was an excellent innovative businessman. He had so much equipment, which needed repairs constantly that he opened up a business called Truck Suppliers, Inc. Its sole purpose was to be able to buy truck parts for his own company at wholesale prices. In order to make it look legitimate for his suppliers, he opened a truck and auto parts store on the edge of his parking lot. The store did so well with the public and the local garages that he then opened several other stores in Virginia and West Virginia.

One of the stockholders of Novick Transfer passed away owning 15 shares of stock. I was given permission to buy the stock and did for $1,500. It has turned out quite well.

The attorney for AJ and I did some estate planning for him and had it all worked out so that his wife would be secure upon his demise. AJ had a heart condition. Unfortunately, his wife was having lunch with friends at the country club, when she dropped dead of a heart attack. There went our estate plan.

AJ started thinking about retiring and selling his company. He was negotiating with a competitor for a $7,000,000 buyout. They got as far as the attorney's office with all the papers drawn and approved by all parties. AJ got up and made a speech about his wonderful company and how lucky the purchaser was to be able to buy his company. After listening to AJ for a while, the president of the buyer got up and said, "You are right AJ you should keep the company." That was the end of the deal and I thought AJ's two sons would shoot their father. The company was eventually sold for substantially less than the original deal. Marshall the elder son went to work for the purchaser and Robert the younger son went off looking for his own way.

Marshall had a very sad experience when Doris, his wife, died from cancer at the age of 27. She was a lovely lady and I had the privilege of knowing her. She was from Easton, Pennsylvania. She left Marshall with three very young children, two girls and a boy. After a period of mourning, Marshall came to New York City, where Novick Transfer had a terminal, and was either introduced to or met Neysa. They married and she moved to Winchester. She was a good mother to the children and an admirable wife to Marshall. The children were so young when their mother died that they must have hardly remembered her.

Marshall had a heart condition also and while driving in Winchester, he suffered a heart attack. He was able to bring his car to a full stop. As luck would have it, an emergency medical person was driving the car behind him and he went to work on Marshall and saved his life at that time.

With Marshall now working for the purchaser of their business, he had to move to New Bedford, Massachusetts with his family. They kept Truck Suppliers going and opened several branch stores in northwest Virginia.

The oldest daughter, Nancy, met and married a Dutch doctor and moved to Holland where she still resides even though she is divorced. The younger daughter, Toby, married and moved to the Denver, Colorado area.

The youngest, Mark was in charge of the Truck Suppliers. Unfortunately Marshall and his wife both passed away at relatively young ages.

When I first started going to Winchester in 1952 it was a sleepy little town with a population of maybe 10,000. Over the years it grew by leaps and bounds. At the beginning Truck Suppliers had no competition from any of the national auto parts stores. As the town grew, at least two nationwide auto parts came to town and the competition became fierce. Mark received an offer from a nationwide firm to purchase the assets of Truck Suppliers and rent the facilities in Winchester. The deal was consummated and Mark went to work for the purchaser. He is still with them as a district manager. Mark and I are very close and we speak to each other at least once a month. He is like an adopted nephew. I continue to prepare the tax returns for the entire family.

Robert, the younger son, called me one-day months later. He asked me to fly down to Baltimore and meet him to look at a pawnshop that was for sale. I could not understand why he would be interested in a small pawnshop. When I got to Baltimore, he took me to the pawnshop. It was a six-story building that occupied an entire city block. Every floor had different merchandise. I reviewed the books and took a tour of the pawnshop. I suggested to Robert that he forget the whole thing. The asking price was excessive, the financial condition was deplorable and the inventory was not moving. He took my advice and went on to buy a Chevrolet Agency. However, I said that if he ever went back to the pawnshop, I would appreciate it if he purchased a decent banjo for me. A few weeks later, I met Bob in New York and here he comes walking towards me with a banjo in his hands tied with a red ribbon. I think I gave him $50 and now my son in law and grandson are playing it.

Connections Pay Off

Talking about Bob Novick. When my middle daughter Amy became 16 we promised to buy her a piano better than the upright piano we had inherited from my mother's aunt. We were looking around for new and used pianos. For some reason, I happened to mention to Bob that we were looking for a piano. He said his mother in law sells pianos in Easton, Pennsylvania and I should call her. He gave me her phone number and I called her. She was a lovely lady and told me that because of my relationship with Bob she would give me a really good price. She could get me a new 5 foot 9 inch Knabe grand piano for which I think the price was $2,300. I said it sounds absolutely great but how could I buy a piano without seeing it. She said for me to just go to East Rochester, New York to view the piano, or I could trust her that we would love what she obtained for us. My wife and I decided to skip the trip to East Rochester, since we would not know what we were looking at anyway as far as the quality of the piano, and we went ahead and ordered the piano. Knabe would not deliver it to my home but would deliver it to a trucking company in New York for delivery to us. Naturally with my trucking connections, I had the piano delivered to one of my trucking clients and they brought it to my home. The piano was packed in a wooden case and the truck men opened the case in the street and assembled the piano in my home. When I called my client to inquire how much I owed them for the delivery, he told me the case that the piano was packed in was one for overseas shipping and was worth more than his charges would be to me.

Amy loved the piano and has it in her home today. After we had the piano for a while it needed tuning. Of course, I had a child prodigy pianist and piano tuner as a client. He had given a concert at Carnegie Hall as a youngster. When he was finished tuning the piano he told us that we must know someone at the Knabe factory because we had a great piano. So trusting Bob's mother in law paid off.

Getting Fleeced

One of the employees of Novick Transport was an ICC practitioner and we were friendly. When AJ sold out, he went into business for himself as an ICC practitioner and was doing well. He called me one day and asked if I would consider being a witness at a case he was conducting in a small town in Pennsylvania. He quoted a daily rate that suited me. We met at his client's office and went over the case. His client had purchased a trucking company and subsequently discovered that he had obligated himself for thousands of dollars which he was not aware of at the time of the purchase. Apparently his accountant was not familiar with the bookkeeping system employed by the over the road trucking industry. Specifically, the seller had not set up an accrual for unpaid employee vacations, union welfare and pensions that had accrued as of the date of the sale of the company. I was placed on the witness stand and explained in very minute detail to the jurors what had taken place and how the buyer had been fleeced. My friend said that I did as good a job as possible and made it as clear as it could be done. Unfortunately, the case was tried in this small town where almost everyone personally knew the owner of the selling company. The verdict came back for the defendant and the jurors said the buyer should have used a more knowledgeable accountant.

Alfred S. owned a luggage store in the Bronx. It had been in his family for many years. My wife and I would pick up his wife in Flushing and we would all go to Al's store on a Saturday evening, wait for him to close the store and then we would go to dinner at a good restaurant at Arthur Avenue. Arthur Avenue was well known to New Yorkers for Italian restaurants.

Al had to close his store in the Bronx as the property was being demolished by the city. He relocated to Madison Avenue in the 40s in I believe what was the Roosevelt Hotel. He took in a partner and had one employee. Al was a very forceful salesman and hated to lose a customer. If his employee was taking care of a customer and did not make the sale, Al would go berserk and scream at the employee that he should have called Al to close the sale. If he made a great sale, he would jump for joy and review with his partner how he fleeced the customer.

My cousin and her friend came from London to visit with us. The friend needed some new luggage and we suggested that she go to see Al, which she did. I had alerted him in advance that they were coming hoping he would take good care of her. The friend purchased some luggage and Al charged her enormous prices for what she had purchased. Shame on him.

Al's company had a sales tax examination. I hate sales tax examinations because they are much worse than IRS exams. I meticulously prepared Al's sales tax returns because I knew that one-day he would have an examination. I had all the backup records available for the auditor. Namely, the sale receipts and purchase invoices. Al sold many pieces of luggage to foreign diplomats and other foreign employees working for embassies. The agent made a list of all the sales to these people because no sales tax was charged for these sales. The agent made another appointment for a couple of weeks hence. He returned and reviewed with me all the non-taxable sales. He had researched the purchaser of each sale and found out that many of the people who had claimed exemption from sales tax had either returned to their native countries before the date of purchase or had not been employed by the embassies for several years. I could not blame Al because he had relied in good faith on the honesty of these customers.

We argued back and forth and although the original proposed assessment was about $15,000, we finally got it down to $4,000. I was prepared to keep fighting to reduce the assessment when Al asked to speak to me. He said for me to stop fighting and he would pay the $4,000 and not to worry because he would retrieve it in the future.

I was not present when the following took place in Al's store. Apparently a customer came to the store and purchased about $800 worth of luggage. He presented Al with a Cashier Check from a New York bank for $1,000. The check looked like it was genuine and Al gave the customer about $200 in change. He deposited the check and about two weeks later, back came the check with a notation "altered amount." The bank sent along the real Cashier Check for $1. This con artist had done a masterful artistic job with a fine ballpoint pen and changed the $1 to $1,000. He had also changed the branch number on the check to another branch of the bank to slow down the process before locating the theft. The con man had purchased at least ten $1 cashier checks and one would think that the bank employee selling the checks should have been slightly suspicious. What amazes me is that someone so artistically talented could not use his creative ability in an honest and legal way.

The hotel was sold to I think the Bank of America and all the stores were told to leave. Al's lease was going to run out in January or February and he would be able to stay for the Christmas selling season. The purchaser of the building put up scaffolding on the entire building that blocked the view of his store. Al mentioned this to his attorney who reviewed in detail Al's lease. Apparently, according to the lease, which had been signed with the hotel, there was a provision prohibiting the placement of scaffolding. The attorney was very clever and got for Al and his partner a handsome settlement from the bank.

Al closed his business and came to me to discuss his future financial outlook. He had two million dollars and was convinced that he would end up a pauper. I told him that I was certain that when he came back to me the following year to prepare his tax return that he would not have dipped into his principal at all. He returned the following year, shaking his head and said that I had been absolutely correct and not only had he not reduced his principal, but had added to it.

After Al went out of business, he revealed to me his coding system. He sold fine expensive leather items and there was a tag on every piece of merchandise but he never told me what the code letters on the tags meant. He now told me that from the codes he knew how much he had paid for the item and if he had purchased it for cash or check. If he had purchased the item for cash, he sold it for cash and pocketed the funds. If he paid for it by check then that sale was entered in the books.

After Al's wife died, he moved to Florida and we heard that he remarried. I lost contact with Al.

Friends Help Increase My Practice

Almost every Friday night I would get together with some friends for a poker game. We would rotate and play at each one's home. The stakes were 5 and 10 cents. We were there not to get rich or become poor but to enjoy each other's company. Two of the players were twins and they owned a photography store on 46th Street west of 5th Avenue. Sammy and Louis would have a fun time in their store. They were identical twins and at times one of them would sell a camera to a customer and then the customer would return the next day to either complain about something or wanted more advice on how to use the camera they had purchased. When the customer would say, "I bought this camera from you yesterday" one of the twins would tell him that he did not purchase it from him and then carry on until finally the other twin would come out to calm down the customer. It worked every time.

They were friendly with and knew Murray, one of the poker players, much longer than they knew me He was an accountant also but they asked me to become their accountant. I did not like the idea of hurting Murray's feelings and I told them that they should speak to Murray.

I started working for them and they were a great source of new clients for me. Their customers were not only walk in trade off the street but an entire array of top-notch professional photographers. The boys always kept their ears peeled to conversations so when the photographers might complain about their current accountants causing them grief for filing their tax returns late or not having filed their tax returns for two or more years and the Internal Revenue was after them. They would suggest to their customers that they contact me to help them. I ended up with an entire array of professional photographers who specialized as sports, movie still, women's fashion and industrial commercial photographers.

If you do not know what a movie still photographer is then let me explain. If you stay in the movie theatre to watch the credits then you will see the title "still photographer" and then some one's name. What the still photographer does is to take photographs when the day's shooting is over of what the set looked like, how each actor was dressed and everything that would be needed so that the next day's shooting follows in exact sequence of where they left off the previous day.

One of the photographers, who became my client during the 1960s, was a freelance photographer for Playboy magazine. His name was Jerry Yulsman, not to be confused with another great photographer by the name of Jerry Ulsman. He was considered to be one of the best technical photographers who taught photography at the New School. We collected his money, paid his bills and doled out the funds for him to live on. At that time my office was located in 1776 Broadway, which was on the corner of 57th Street and Broadway. Sometimes he would show up at the office, out of breath, needing $20 to pay off the cab that was waiting downstairs.

On two different occasions he used me as a model and I appeared in Playboy. I still have the magazines to prove my modeling career. I told you accounting could be fun. The first modeling appearance was that I was dressed as a New York City policeman. The theme for the photo shoot was Shakespearean. It took place on a frigid Sunday morning in February. The location was on 25th Street on the East Side in front of a courthouse. Men placed themselves at each end of the street and blocked traffic. The woman model that was hired for the shoot decided not to show up. Jerry, the photographer went to his little metal box containing 3 by 5 index cards with the face of the model stapled to the card. He called another model and she showed up in a few minutes in a cab. The model had to pose bare breasted carrying a protest sign and the caption under the picture that appeared in Playboy read "she doff protest too much". The model showed up practically nude wearing a mink coat. She removed the coat, the pictures were shot, she put the coat back on and she and I got into a car to warm up. She turned to me, extended her hand to me and said, "I do not think we have been properly introduced." I loved it. In the picture I am the cop on the right.

The next time I was called on to display my modeling acumen I was to pose as a black marketer during the Second World War. I was dressed in a zoot suit, a fedora and smoking a big black cigar. I was seated in a large club chair surrounded by about four naked women and one woman, who was dressed, who was supposed to be my moll. She had a leg up on the club chair and I had to place my hand on her leg. She turned to me and said, "Don't look up my skirt." That was the height of being ridiculous. In addition to the women, I was surrounded by cartons of cigarettes, meat, silk stockings and sugar. All of which were in short supplies during the war.

The man in charge of the shoot was a Japanese gentleman, the head photo editor of Playboy. The second shooting had to be done all over again. There were cartons of Lucky Strike cigarettes in the picture and were the color green, which was Lucky Strike's color. But, during the war Lucky Strike's green had gone to war and the cartons were white. So we went through the whole thing again. I got paid $250 for each time I did the modeling. When my friends saw the magazines, they all wanted to get into the act.

I requested from Playboy magazines permission to include the two pictures in this book but they refused because the photographs contained naked women. I always thought that naked women was what Playboy magazines was all about. In the event any of my readers want to see the photographs you can go online and locate the October 1966 edition and find page 137 and the November 1967 edition and find page 105.

I was already a father at that time and one of my youngest daughter's friends came to visit and my daughter showed her the photo in which I was posing as a policeman. The children were innocence personified. My daughter's friend said, "I didn't know your father was a policeman."

Jerry, the photographer was given a choice to move to Chicago and go on staff at Playboy or end his relationship with the magazine. He decided to stay in New York. He went on to do all sorts of work and then became the photographer for the Barnum and Bailey Circus.

When we moved from New York City to Great Neck, Jerry was the only client I lost. He could not take a cab to Great Neck to collect $20.

One of the still photographers was Louis Goldman. He worried every day of his life about when he was going to get the next job. He was a survivor of the Holocaust. He was hidden in France in a convent for several years. His family had moved to Israel. He did not have to serve in the army because a brother had been killed in one of the wars in Israel. My wife and I visited with his mother in Tel Aviv on one of our visits to Israel. She was a lovely woman but spoke no English. We communicated in French, German and Yiddish and got along famously. She prepared a delicious dinner for us. She eventually made a trip to New York and we repaid the hospitality.

Louis lived in a rent-controlled apartment on the East River. He could keep the apartment as long as his income did not exceed a certain income level. I prepared his return, which he filed. He then went to H&R Block and had a return prepared which he submitted to the rental authority. Unfortunately, Louis died of a heart attack while on the job out west. The producer dedicated the movie to him and there was a eulogy at the end of the film.

Another photographer is a famous sport photographer named Ken R. His photos have appeared in Sports Illustrated and other sports magazines. When he became my client he was in partnership with Roy, an Englishman. Roy wanted to run a photo agency representing other photographers but Ken wanted to shoot pictures. Their relationship ended badly and they almost came to blows. Roy moved to California and they parted company. I kept them both as clients.

Over and above the sports photos taken by Ken, he also did still photography and got assignments for all sorts of work. He won the international press photographer's award one-year for a photo that he took in Russia at the Kremlin. It is a picture of the back of Ted Kennedy with his arm around his son, who had recently lost his leg from cancer. Ken has had a very close relationship with the Kennedy family. I have the picture hanging on the wall of my office.

My partner Freddy begged to take over Ken's account because it was so exciting to be in his studio. Freddy's been doing his work ever since and has accumulated several of Ken's friends and associates as clients.

Roy, as I said, moved to California with his wife. He took pictures of the movie stars and also represented other photographers. My wife and I were vacationing in California and of course we visited Roy and Jean, his wife. They took us to dinner in a restaurant, whose name I think was Dantan. In the restaurant, sitting opposite us was Groucho Marx and several of his guests. Groucho was wearing a topcoat and was obviously cold. Several tables away sat Burgess Meredith. For those not old enough to remember Burgess; he acted in many movies, just look for his name in some of the oldies. After a while Groucho got up to relieve himself and stopped to chat with Burgess Meredith. While on his way back to his table from the men's room, I could not pass up the opportunity of a lifetime to say something to Groucho. When he got in front of our table, I said, "excuse me Groucho, but what brand of cigars do you smoke?" This was so many years ago that people were still smoking cigars in restaurants and I am a cigar smoker. Groucho actually stopped and chatted with us. He said that there was no point telling me what kind of cigars he smoked because I couldn't afford them. He then went on to talk with us and asked us if we were going to see his one man show. I told him that we would be heading back to New York but our friends lived in Los Angeles and they might see the show. Groucho said the show would be sold out and I told Groucho that with his connections he could get our friends in. Groucho said, "I haven't been in myself in years." Unfortunately, Groucho died before he did his one-man show.

I think it was about a year or two later that Roy and Jean were passing through New York on their way to the Cannes Film Festival. I went to visit them at their hotel. They had sold their home in California and would have no place to return to. Roy asked me if I would help him draft a will for himself. I am not an attorney but we took some paper and pen and we wrote a simple will wherein he left everything to his wife. I think we asked a couple of the hotel employees to witness the will.

Roy and Jean went onto Cannes and while there he suffered a heart attack. Jean got him to a hospital but he passed away. Jean was distraught and had a tremendous amount of difficulty getting the body to England where she wanted to bury him. Obviously Roy must have been told by his doctor that his time was very limited and that is why he had me help him with his will.

Eventually Jean returned to the United States. She came to stay with us since she had no other place to go. She stayed a few months. Even though, she had no home to return to in California she did not want to stay in New York. She had friends in California and she and I got on a plane and I took her back to Los Angeles to be with her friends until she could rebuild her life.

Roy has been dead for many years now, but Jean is still selling his photos and receives unsolicited fees from foreign magazines all over the world that use his photos in their magazines. Jean has learned how to handle a camera and has become a photographer on her own. She has also become the executive director of the foreign press organization that sponsors the Golden Globe Awards. She travels the world for them and attends film openings. Her assignments bring her to New York occasionally. She took my wife and me to a film opening of a 007 film with Pierce Brosnan. He spotted Jean in the audience and went out of his way to say hello to her and she introduced us to him. Jean continues to be a friend and client and we see her whenever she comes to New York if she has the time.

One of the people introduced by the camera store boys was a Chinese lady. She was a cinematographer. She was short and heavyset but she carried the heavy movie cameras on the job. She came to my office in Manhattan one time with her father. She and her father sat in front of my desk and conversed with each other in French. She later told me that her father had been Chang Kai-Shek's minister to Paris for several years. She stupidly bought an expensive movie camera at a large discount price. It needed repair and she brought it in for a repair. When she went to pick it up she was told that the camera had been stolen from them and she lost all her money. Obviously she was foolish and learned an expensive lesson.

Once again, the boys recommended a potential client. She was not a professional photographer but photography was her hobby and she also used it in her job. She was an editor for an art magazine. I met with Susan and was engaged by her. I prepared her tax returns for a while and we discussed her job and her ambitions. I strongly suggested to Susan that she take a chance like I had done, quit her job and break out on her own. She hesitated for a while but eventually started her own business. She had written a book called "Designing With Type". It is an excellent book and a standard for graphic designers and is still bringing her royalties every year. She had excellent contacts in the publishing field and began representing authors. She became a book packager. What that means is that with her connections she would approach a publisher with an idea for a book and an outline. If the publisher liked the idea, they would give her an advance and she would hire the author, the artist, the editor, the proofreader, the photographer and anyone else needed to produce the book. She would then deliver to the publisher the finished galleys or in some instances the actual books. The reason the publishers would engage her rather than produce the books in house is that with Susan's knowledge and pricing, the publishers would know the absolute cost. She is really talented and her business grew and grew. She joined forces with Marsha, another brilliant lady and things continued on.

They produced books for Crayola, Disney, American Express and many others. They produced for American Express a book instructing women about what to do if they ran into problems while driving their cars. The book was in the shape of a folded map, about five inches by ten inches. It was a success and they were collecting their fees and royalties. Until one day a woman called their office and inquired if she could purchase a book directly from them, since their company's name was on the books. They asked this woman how she purchased her first book and she told them. It turned out that American Express had not revealed to Susan and Marsha they had printed thousands of books on their own. When confronted they said, "oh yes we were going to get around to tell you". So much for ethics. They did collect what was due to them.

After a number of years they took in a third partner. Another very bright young lady. I advised them to sell her a portion of the business. They did not listen to my advice and learned later to regret that they did not. Susan and Marsha have retired and although Susan did get bought out, Marsha was not that fortunate and the young lady reaped a huge reward.

Sarah L. is successful literary agent. I sent her the first few chapter of this book for her review and suggestions. She liked my story telling and said that she wished her dad had done the same thing. Sarah did not think there was any commercial value to my book in today's market, not that I have any aspirations of my own. She suggested I complete the book for my family and friends and told me to contact Patty Bashe Romanoski to help me. I did listen and Patty has been a great help.

Ruth S., my "financial advisor", recommended Debbie M. to me. Debbie is a highly successful executive and the president of a large graphic design company. Their offices are in the Empire State Building. The showroom is full of the products they have designed for some of the largest companies in this country. The boxes, containers, etc are all for very familiar household products that are well known to all of us. She has written at least two books that I know of and teaches and travels throughout the country.

I Am Accused Of Practicing Law

My friend, Leonard Davis, the founder of AARP had a friend who knew the automotive parts business. He loaned Edward A. sufficient funds to get started. Edward eventually opened a half a dozen automotive parts stores all along Hempstead Turnpike in Nassau County. All the stores were on the south side of the street in order to attract the do it yourselfers on their way home at night. The name of the company was DACO Automotive. Obvious the DA was for Davis's assistance in getting him started. I became the accountant to protect Davis's investment. Edward slowly paid off the debt to Davis and when it was all paid, Leonard Davis turned over his shares in the company to Edward. A very nice gesture and I am sure that Davis had loaned funds to others that never repaid him.

After Edward was in business for a few years, his company was written up in a trade publication. The publications mistakenly called the business DAYCO Automotive. Shortly after the release of the publication, Edward received a letter from the DAYCO Rubber Company, which was listed on the New York Stock Exchange. The letter directed Edward to immediately change the name of his company because he was infringing on their name. Edward consulted with his attorney. The attorney requested a $5,000 retainer fee to fight for Edward to keep the name. Fortunately, it was the time of the month for me to be at Edward's place of business for my monthly review of his records. Even though Edward was amenable to sending the $5,000 to the attorney, he had not mailed it as yet. I read the letter from the DAYCO Rubber Company and picked up the phone and called the gentleman who had written the letter. I told him I was associated with the DACO Company and that the publication made an error in the spelling of our name. He said it made no difference; we must change our name because it was still too similar to their name. I told him that it was too bad that he had not written a few weeks earlier because we had just painted our fleet of trucks, printed brochures and lettered all the windows in all our stores. If he would send us $100,000 we would gladly change our name. He said, "No way" and he would begin suit. At which point I asked him, "Were you not previously called the Dayton Rubber Company." He admitted that and when he discovered that we were incorporated as DACO before they changed their name to DAYCO, it was the end of the conversation. You never heard such insults against me when the attorney found out what I had done. He accused me of practicing law and cried about losing his fee. So you see that there is more to accounting than addition and subtraction. I do not know why I remembered the change of name from Dayton Rubber to DAYCO but it just popped into my mind at that time.

John Russell was a banker with the now defunct Franklin National Bank. He was the banker for DACO and we got to know him intimately. We prepared his tax returns and of course, in anticipation that he might recommend clients to us, we never sent him a bill for our services. He always offered to pay but we refused to accept anything from him. After preparing his returns for several years, we failed to hear from him. On April 14th he called our office and asked if he could please come to see us. He was embarrassed that he had not been able to pay for our services and had gone to H&R Block to prepare his tax returns. John likes to talk and he told us that every time he opened his mouth to the employee at H&R Block, the employee reached behind him and grabbed another schedule. When the tax return was finally completed, John found out that he owed hundreds of dollars in additional taxes. The fee was in excess of $300 and included all the schedules for which there were separate fees. This was more than twenty years ago. John pleaded with us to help him. We reviewed the tax returns he showed us, corrected the errors and prepared new returns. John ended up owing just a few dollars. We then charged him a very nominal fee and he stayed with us until his demise.

My Smaller Trucking Company Clients

One of the smaller trucking companies that I had as a client was what I called a trucking-less trucking company. Pasquale, known as Pat and Cosmo were brothers who owned this company that operated out of a store on Ninth Avenue in the 30s. The large tractor-trailers are not allowed to drive into the garment center in Manhattan. The tractors would pull up to my client's place of business early in the morning, and unload hundreds of rolls of piece goods. They would place the piece goods on hand trucks and rolling wagons and carts and deliver the piece goods to the clothing manufacturers in the garment center. In the late afternoon the process would be reversed. They would go into the garment center, place the finished garments in the same vehicles and bring them back to the store. The tractors would pick up the finished garments for delivery to stores all over the county.

The bookkeeper was Benny Calamari, also known as Benny the Squid. There was no room on the ground floor of the store for an office; so, they built an office on a balcony with a staircase leading up to the office. One day while I was working there, the bosses had fired one of the Latino help for insubordination. He left and returned in a little while with a gun. Shots were fired and Benny and I saw bullets coming up through the floor in the office. Fortunately, John, a huge black man, grabbed the shooter and wrestled him to the ground. This was all in day's work—boy were we scared.

Pat had reasons sometimes to come to my home to pick me up and drive me to work with him. He loved my wife and always showed up with coffee, bagels and cake. They eventually did go into the trucking business and expanded their business. Pat and I went to an attorney's office at 39 Broadway. Pat was to buy the trucking business from another client of mine. During the negotiations, Pat turned to me and said he had to go to the men's room and would I go with him. I said I do not have to go but he said he wanted to talk. So, I accompanied him to the john. We were both standing at the urinals relieving ourselves when a black man came out of one of the stalls. He had a newspaper tucked under his arm and went to wash his hands. When Pat and I were finished we turned around to see this man with a huge knife in his hands. He demanded our money and jewelry. I gave him the money I had but as it turned out I had three new $100.00 bills, which were folded flat in my pocket and even though he frisked us, he did not feel these new bills. I had no intention of not giving him all my money but I just did not feel the three bills when I went to empty my pocket. He took from me a gold Omega watch that I had just recently purchased in Israel and my wallet. He told us to get into the stalls. I went in, climbed up on the toilet seat and locked the door. He took a paper towel, placed my wallet on it and slid it under the door. He was not interested in credit cards. Of course he warned us to stay inside the men's room for 10 minutes because he would be standing outside waiting for us. I was kind of shocked that Pat had been so docile and I thought for sure that he would tackle with the thief, but was a pussycat just like me.

We went back into the attorney's office and told them what happened. They thought we were kidding but when they saw the blood drained out of our faces, they knew we were not kidding. They called the police and they showed up inside of two minutes. This thief had been robbing people for some time and obviously had a great hiding place in the building. They showed us an artist's conception of what the thief looked like that was developed from a previous person who had been attacked. It was a great likeness. Since I had just recently purchased the watch in Israel and had declared it as I went through customs, I had the serial number and gave it to the police. I figured that was the last I was ever going to see the watch.

Weeks later, I was working at a dress shop client in Bronxdale, New York. I got a call from the police that they think they caught the thief and I had to come down to Slip Street Station to identify the man. I told the police that I was miles away and since he had robbed so many people, there must be someone else they could call. They said there was no one else to call and I had to come. So, I drove all the way down to the southern part of Manhattan. Unlike the TV programs showing people looking through a one-way mirror to view a lineup of several people and then you were supposed to pick out the criminal. They led me to a door with a peephole and I looked through the hole to see a black man sitting on a stool. I asked them to tell him to stand up. The man was about six feet two inches. I told the policeman that the thief was about five foot nine inches and why were they wasting my time. The policeman said that perhaps he was slouching when he attacked us.

As it turned out, the man in the room was the person who had pawned my watch. A few days later, I got a call from the police telling me that they thought they found my watch. I was to go to a pawnshop in Brooklyn, with a friend. We went to Brooklyn and my friend sat in the car with the motor running while I went into the pawnshop. I told the proprietor that the police had sent me. He did not say a word and went to his huge safe, took out an envelope. He tore open the envelope and there lo and behold was my watch. I told him that it was my watch and again he said nothing. Put the watch back in the envelope and back it went in the safe. Eventually I got the watch back. That episode took place about thirty years ago and I am still wearing the watch.

While they had their business on Ninth Avenue, a competitor opened up a few doors away doing exactly the same type of business. Cosmo had five sons. Unfortunately one of his sons died as a teenager from cancer. One of his sons ultimately became a preacher and ended up a drunk and committed suicide. Although Cosmo was Italian and was raised Catholic, he became a born again Christian as did the son who became a minister.

One of his sons decided to put the competition out of business. One night, I believe on a weekend, the son and a friend broke into the competitor's place of business and poured gasoline all over the floor. This occurred in the wee hours of the morning. Thank goodness a police patrol car came along and spotted the sole car parked on Ninth Avenue and went to investigate. They caught the bad boys preparing to ignite the entire building. There were tenement apartments above the store and there is no telling how many people would have burned to death had the police not happened along. In addition the son and his cohort had their shoes and pant legs soaked with gasoline and probably would have set themselves on fire. Cosmo had not sent his son to do the deed and ended up paying a fortune in legal fees. I forget if the son went to jail.

Eventually Cosmo and Pat parted company and Cosmo went on to really go into the trucking business. He kept me on as the accountant. The trucking company was located in Jersey City and basically did the same type of trucking as Yale Transport. They were successful for a while until they lost their largest customer. I had periodically prepared financial statements for the corporation. I prepared a statement showing a substantial loss and sent it to Cosmo. Sometime later I got a call from a banker who wanted to review my financial statement with me because the trucking company was requesting a rather large loan. I told him to hold on while I went to get my copy of the report. What he read off had no relationship to the statement I had prepared and I told him so. I faxed a copy of my statement to him and that was the last I heard of it. Cosmo had a man working for him, who thought that he knew bookkeeping and accounting. He had taken my stationery and reproduced it on the copy machine and had prepared a ridiculous financial report that made absolutely no sense. The profit and loss statement showed a huge profit but did not coordinate with the balance sheet. Obviously Cosmo was thrown out of that bank but this scheme was something cooked up by his sons and the alleged bookkeeper. Cosmo apologized to me and I stayed on to represent him.

I always had my desk to work at when I went to Jersey City. One time when I came to work, my desk was covered with cartons. Cosmo was in Florida, so I went into his office and began my work at his desk. I was not in there five minutes when the phone rang. It was Cosmo calling from Florida. He said, "I understand that you are sitting at my desk" which I acknowledged. He then said, "There are things on my desk that you may not want to see." I said, "Cosmo, I am moving right now."

After a while Cosmo decided to retire and he told me that he was sure that once he was gone his boys would want their own accountant. I told him that when he leaves I would not want to stay on. Eventually his sons failed and one or more ended up in jail.

Cosmo was married to Carmela. Carmela was not very mentally swift. One day while I was working at Cosmo's trucking company, he received a call from his wife and he immediately got dressed and prepared to leave. I asked him what happened and he told me that his wife had stuck her head in the oven and lit the oven and burned off all the hair on her head.

Carmela subsequently needed a great deal of dental work. She apparently insisted that it should all be done in one session. She went to the dentist, who also had an anesthesiologist working with him. They administered the anesthetic and Carmela stopped breathing for a short time. They brought her back to life but the damage was already done. Carmela lost most of her sight and she became legally blind. Cosmo is a fabulous person at times and took excellent care of his wife. Cosmo, his wife and me and my wife attended a formal occasion. Cosmo had dressed his wife, applied makeup to her face and combed her hair most attractively.

Obviously, Cosmo engaged an attorney and he sued for the damage done to his wife. The case dragged on for quite some time and eventually it was given a court date. The trial proceeded for several days and just before it went to the jury, the insurance company made an offer of $400,000 during a lunch break. Cosmo's attorney told him to turn down the offer because he was certain that the jury would award him at least one million dollars. Well, things did not turn out well. The jury came back with a decision for the defendant. Cosmo was awarded nothing, zero, zilch, and nada.

The insurance company had done their research and had learned that Carmela's driver's license had been recently renewed. I am sure that with Cosmo's "connections" he had gotten a letter from an optician stating that Carmela has passed the required eye exam. It was absolutely stupid on his part because with her failing eyesight, she was never going to get any better and she would never drive again. In addition, we found out later that one of the jurors had said that anyone, who could afford $4,000 for dental work, got what they deserved. So, the jurors must have felt that she was lying about her eyesight and of course Cosmo could not say that he had bribed an optician.

Cosmo was livid with his attorney and with himself for listening to his advice. I guess it all boiled down to greed on his part and the lawyer.

Friends Pass The CPA Examination

One of my friends, Murray L. struggled for about twenty year to finally pass the CPA exam. Another mutual friend, Milton H. struggled alongside Murray and they both never gave up the ghost. They studied diligently together for years. Unfortunately, the CPA exam consists of four parts and even though you may pass one or two of the parts, you must pass them pass them all with a certain time frame, or you lose the ones you have passed. I am not certain that the same rules are still in effect. That is what happened to these two gentlemen. They must have had to take some of the parts of the exam at least twice. But, I give them a great deal of credit for perseverance and they both eventually became CPAs. The minute my wife and I heard that Murray passed the exam, we grabbed a bottle of champagne and drove to Murray's home to celebrate with him and his wife.

Murray called me one day and asked if I would be interested in representing a client of his before the Internal Revenue Service, because he did not feel comfortable representing this individual. I told him to have this man call me and I would speak to him. The man came to my office and confessed that he had been found guilty of assisting people feloniously to receive social security payments. Obviously, he was working for the social security administration and got caught with his hand in the cookie jar. We did not discuss what jail time he might be facing for what he done, but we did discuss what the Internal Revenue Service now wants from him. He showed me the tax returns he had prepared for himself and on the face of it; it appeared that there was not much to be concerned with, other than the fact that he had not reported as income the bribes he had received. He was single, lived with his sister, and claimed her as a dependent. He told me that he paid all the expenses for their household and supported his sister. I told him that I would do the best I could for him and asked for a retainer of a few thousand dollars. He came prepared and gave me what I had requested in cash. Needless to say, the retainer was deposited the very next morning in our business account.

I arranged a meeting at the Internal Revenue and he accompanied me to the meeting. The IRS agent who greeted us was in the legal department of the IRS and he already knew of the man's indiscretions at the social security administration. The agent asked my client if he had gone to college. I interceded and asked if that was pertinent? I was told to sit down and let my client answer the question. Well, he had gone to college and therefore I assume that he was educated and not particularly stupid.

The agent had stacks of folders in front of him. It appeared that the IRS had circularized every bank and stock brokerage firm in the metropolitan area asking about my client. They had received replies detailing all the accounts he had and the interest, dividends and stock transactions that had not been reported on his tax returns. My client had advised me previously that he had omitted substantial income, but again this was before the issuance of forms 1099. The client admitted freely the errors of his ways and we proceeded with the examination.

The agent then referred to the sister, whom he had claimed as a dependent. He showed us a tax return prepared for the sister, who apparently had been working. The returns were prepared with a pen. The agent asked the client if the handwriting on the sister's tax return was his. He admitted that he had prepared the tax returns for the sister.

At this point, I addressed myself to the tax agent and said that up to this point the client had admitted everything to me about what he had omitted from his tax return, but he had never told me about his stupidity about preparing his sister's tax returns and at the same time claiming her as a dependent. I said, "If you don't mind, at this point I feel that there is nothing I can do to help this client and I am leaving." The agent said that it is all right with him if I felt that I wanted to leave and I did. I had gotten paid for my endeavors and I never heard from the client or the IRS again in this matter.

And you thought accounting was dull and boring. I did not run into too many nuts in my time, but this one took the cake.

Cosmo Becomes A Source Of Clients.

Larry S loves to tell the story about what happened to him when he was in grade school. Apparently a classmate took ill in the classroom. The teacher tried calling the boy's mother and found out that she only spoke Italian. The teacher, so Larry tells it, asked if any of the students spoke Italian. Larry raised his hand and the teacher handed him the phone. Larry swears that the conversation went like this. "Mrs. Scaduto this is Larry, your sona hesa sicka and you betta coma quicka to taka hima homa." Knowing Larry as I do, he is probably telling the absolute truth.

Larry S is a nephew of Cosmo and he worked for him for several years. Then they had an altercation and Larry left to go into business for himself. Larry is a smart young man and succeeded in the trucking business. He ran a trucking company and also went into the warehouse end of it. He rented a couple of huge warehouses in New Jersey. He would store the rolls of fabric brought up from the textile mills in the south. He had an elaborate computer system to identify each roll of fabric and when the manufacturers in the garment center would call for the delivery of specific rolls of fabric, Larry's boys would locate the rolls and deliver them.

This worked out well for quite a time until the garment center disappeared from Manhattan and Larry had to close his doors as a wealthy man. Larry as well as Cosmo were born Catholics but they converted to Born Again Christians. Larry supported a small church in Staten Island and always wanted to get Fred and me into conversations about the New Testament.

Cosmo suggested to a fellow parishioner that he call me. Andy R. did call and I went to work for him. He and his son in law manufactured lamps. The factory was in Brooklyn. They sold their products to department stores. The factory appeared to be completely disoriented and they struggled to stay afloat. After a couple of years, Andy, who was now over 65 decided to retire and turned the business over to the son in law. He went to the Social Security office to file for his benefits. The social security employees are always very suspicious of applicants who owned their own business and are now claiming that they are no longer working. I should have gone with Andy, but he never asked me to go with him. They gave him a very hard time but they eventually approved his application. I had written a letter testifying that Andy was legitimately unemployed.

One day, Andy came into the shop, just to visit and as luck would have it, an investigator from the Social Security came to check up on Andy to see if he was really retired. When he found Andy on the premises, he assumed that Andy was still working. That incident cost Andy his social security checks for quite a while.

The son in law was not a good businessman and failed within a short period of time. The one saving feature was that I was able to acquire two antique hutches before they closed their doors. I refinished both of them and gave one to my daughter Amy.

Lenny Fialkow Finally Does Something Nice.

My "friend" Lenny was doing so well, financially, at AARP that he decided to give up the couple of clients that he had on his own. He turned them over to me. One of the businesses was on the northwest corner of 14th Street and 9th Avenue. It was on the second floor and occupied the entire floor, which was almost an entire city block. What they did was to wash, steam, and dye fabrics for the garment trade. It was a substantial business run by two brothers and a brother in law. The brother in law, Abe, was believe it or not both a dentist and a Certified Public Accountant. Obviously a strange combination! The dentistry had come first. He did the bookkeeping and production records.

Directly across the street was the restaurant Old Homestead, known for its meat, since they were in the meat district. Many times we would go to lunch there.

Again, with the diminishing of the garment center in New York, their business began to shrink and finally it got to the point where it made no sense to try to buck the tide and they closed their doors. I am sure that the space they occupied is now several spacious expensive apartments.

The other client that was turned over to me from Lenny was a supplier of industrial cleaning products. They operated in New Jersey. It was a husband and wife affair, small but profitable. After some time they decided to move their operation to Sag Harbor, New York where they owned a home. They opened up a shop on the main street and became a Montgomery Ward catalog shop. I would travel to Sag Harbor once a year to obtain their records. It was an all day adventure. The Long Island Expressway did not exist at yet. They were nice people and the wife was very bright but unfortunately was mentally unstable. She committed suicide and he just could not go on without her and closed his doors.

Nat Sheinman Passed Away But His Legacy

Continued On.

Bert R. is the nephew of Nat Sheinman. His mother was Nat's sister. I have been like an uncle to him and we have remained close probably for 40 years or more. He has recommended friends of his from time to time to become my clients. These friends are artistic and clever men who have succeeded in their endeavors.

One of his friends, and now a client is John K. John is a brilliant graphic artist and runs a successful operation. He has designed brochures for IBM, greeting cards for the Museum of Modern Art and a variety of other items for some of the largest companies in this country. A Japanese client came to John, from a recommendation. They were opening stores in many parts of Japan to sell only American made merchandise. I guess they felt that "made in the U. S. A." would sell in Japan. John suggested that they call their stores "Johnny K" and they loved the idea. John's last name begins with a K. He designed for them their stationery, shopping bags, advertising material and a host of other items to be used by them. They were very happy with what John had accomplished for them and invited him to come to Japan, at their expense, to the opening of one of their stores. Of course John went and had a grand time and was well treated. They put him up in one of the finest hotels and sometime during the night, came a knock on the door. When he opened the door he saw a lovely Japanese maiden who told him that she was sent to entertain him for the night. Foolishly John sent her away and that was the last he heard from his Japanese client. John has now gone into becoming an artist as well as a graphic artist and is doing well. He had a showing at a gallery in Sag Harbor, New York and did well. I love John and John loves my family and me.

Another of Bert's friends, who also became a client, was Rick. Rick was born in Montreal and still had family in Canada. He liked living in New York and had a one-bedroom apartment on Central Park West. His claim to fame was that Jerry Seinfeld lived in the same apartment house. Rick ran his business from his apartment and in all the months that I visited Rick's office, I never spotted Jerry Seinfeld.

I do not know how Rick ended up in the business that he had. Perhaps he was a salesman in the industry before going into business for himself. I never thought to ask. In any event, Rick sold children's T-shirts. He would either have artists design the T-shirts or would buy expensive shirts by another manufacturer and then copy their designs with slight alterations. He never touched the products that he had manufactured for him. He bought the blank shirts and had them sent to shops that would paint, flock and put sparkles, etc on the shirts. Then the products would be shipped directly to his customers. Rick sold only to large chain stores and did about four million dollars in sales annually.

As with many of my clients, Rick and I became very close. He would drop in at my house in the Hamptons and come with a bag of bagels, lox, cream cheese and pastries. He loved my wife Frances and she loved him.

Rick purchased the small apartment adjoining his apartment and then broke down the connecting wall to make a lovely spacious apartment. While the construction was going on, Rick moved his operation to an office in the garment center. Rick's sole employee was Lori S. Lori sold the products and did the record keeping for the flow of the merchandise from the initial purchase of the blank shirts to the final products and traced the shipping to customers.

For some unknown reason Rick became seriously ill. We knew he was gay, but I do not think he had AIDS. Lori tried nursing him back to health. Not only did she work for him for years, but also she adored him. Sadly, Rick passed away in his apartment in the arms of Lori. I do not think she will ever get over that. Sometime after the funeral, Lori arranged a memorial service in a restaurant for his friends and business associates. My wife and I attended and I made a short eulogy for my friend.

Rick had two brothers in Canada. One, I believe was a brother and the other a half brother. The brother is an attorney practicing in Montreal. Of course he came to New York for the funeral and then returned to address the estate left by Rick. He was able to sell the apartment for about one million dollars. He then contacted me to deal with the business. I prepared a balance sheet and profit and loss statement for the business as of the date of Rick's demise. I then met with the brother and discussed with him the best method of winding down the business. He knew of Lori's position with the company. At this point my loyalty was strictly with Lori. I explained to him that he has two choices. One would be to take over the company himself. The other choice was for him to appeal to Lori to stay on and wind up the affairs.

I told him that if Lori left now, he would not know where to collect the $800,000 in accounts receivable, nor would he know which supplier had to be paid. However, if Lori were to stay then she would collect the receivables, liquidate the payables and turn over to him the net proceeds. I insisted that if he wanted Lori to do this for him, then he would then have to turn the stock in the company over to Lori for $1. He agreed to my terms, since he had no choice. A legal document was drawn up specifically detailing all that was agreed to by the two parties. Lori did for him all that I promised she would do and the brother ended up with a small fortune. He just did not have the brains to give Lori a bonus for her endeavors.

Lori was happy to acquire the company. She was very apprehensive about designing new products, as it was something she had never done before. I worked with her and she learned very quickly what her customers wanted. She paid designers, bought some samples and proceeded to run the business. With the downturn in business in general, her sales are not quite what Rick achieved, but she is capable of drawing a decent salary for herself. She has working for her a talented young lady, Lucia, who assists her in running her business. Lori is close to the buyers working for her customers and has a fabulous relationship with them. She and I have a wonderful relationship and I do all I can to help her and take care of her needs.

One of her largest customers was Kohl's Department Stores. She sold them about $2,000,000 worth of merchandise each year. Suddenly, their buyer must have gone to China and for a few pennies less per garment, she lost them completely as a customer.

The Internal Revenue Reviews My Tax Returns.

Obviously, for the many years that I have been a practicing accountant, I have had the necessity to represent my clients before the Internal Revenue Service. There are some clients that I trust to take with me and some clients I discourage from coming with me because they might say the wrong things. In addition, if the client is not with me then I can kind of hedge my bets and tell the agent that I do not know the answer and that I will get them the answer at our next meeting, which I cannot do if the client is with me.

In 1967 my eldest daughter came down with Hodgkin's disease and I had tremendous medical expenses. I was called to the Flushing office of the IRS to have my 1967 tax return reviewed. I parked outside the office and put a couple of quarters in the meter, assuming that I would be out within an hour. I had all my documentation stapled together with adding machine tapes for each category such as my medical expenses, real estate taxes, mortgage interest and contributions. I got an elderly Jewish lady as the inquisitor.

She took all my documentation, ripped off the adding machine tapes, discarded them in the trash bin and removed the staples and spread all my records all over her desk. I told her that the reason for the large medical expenses was because of my daughter's illness. She slowly and meticulously went through every paid invoice and corresponding cancelled check.

Then she got to my contributions. She wanted to know why some of my contributions were either for $18 or multiples of $18. She wanted to know if these checks were for show tickets? I said to her, "you are Jewish aren't you so you must know that $18 is Chai and that it is usually a symbol for life and Jewish people commonly make donations in multiples of $18." She turned to a contribution I had made to the Red Cross equivalent in Israel. She told me that it is not an allowable contribution. I told that it definitely was deductible. She got out of her seat and went to the back of the room. Apparently it was her group chief's office. She looked at a book that is about six inches thick that contains every organization that is recognized by the IRS as a charitable deduction. She came back to me and said that the contribution was in fact deductible.

She then went through the balance of my contributions and twice more she went back to her boss's office to refer to his book. The last time she went, I could almost hear him telling her to stop coming back to him and that each of the contributions I was claiming is deductible. At this point, I had to go to my car and put another couple of quarters in the meter.

She kept me for a total of a little over two hours, for an examination that should have taken about 15 minutes. At the end of my ordeal, she turned to me and said and I quote, "I guess I will have to accept your return as you filed it." I said, "Is that so strange?" To which she replied that it has never happened to her before.

Another interesting tax examination comes to mind. Jack S. and Irving S. and I were fishing buddies. Irving was a cousin of mine by marriage and he and Jack were friends and co-workers at a company that produced drapery and upholstery fabrics. Irving worked in the office on the converting records and Jack was an outside salesman. I prepared their personal tax returns, although I did not charge Irving.

Jack was a legitimate outside travelling salesman. He made three trips a year to Michigan, Louisiana and Florida and traveled by car. He earned a decent living and it was hard work but he loved it. Many trips he took his wife with him.

He was called for a tax examination and I took his shopping bag full of toll tickets, gasoline receipts, and hotel and motel receipts with me to the IRS. The assigned agent was an intelligent young man. We had a discussion relative to Jack's occupation and style of living. He then asked me if I had a newspaper to read while he went through the shopping bag. I must have sat there for almost an hour when he returned with his notes and the shopping bag. His head was shaking from side to side and he said that he had traced each of the trips taken by Jack and all the receipts were in proper sequence of events. We both agreed that most people who contend to be travelling salesman are not what they claim to be in spite of the items they claim on their tax returns.

The agent told me that Jack would get a clean bill of health. However, before I leave, would I give him permission to photocopy a few of the cancelled checks? I told him to be my guest.

He returned in a few minutes and I inquired about what he had done. The cancelled checks that he had photocopied were three checks to Jack's wife's doctor. He showed me the front of checks payable to Dr Jones and the endorsement on the back of the checks of the ABC Pharmacy. The doctor had been cashing each of these checks at the pharmacy. I told this story to a friend of mine who owned a pharmacy in Manhattan and he said this procedure goes on each and every day in his store. I do not envy the doctor when he gets called down for an examination of his return.

CLIENT MAKES A FOOLISH DECISION

My list of clients goes on. This one was at the corner of Grand Street and Broadway in Manhattan. Again, a very interesting business. They sold parts for printing presses. These parts were needed for the very old printing presses normally being used in small printing shops throughout the world. They had an inventory of parts that no one else had and if a printer needed a part then they had to come to this supplier. The owners were two brothers, Harold and Julius who had been in this business all of their working lives. They occupied a sizeable area consisting of the entire ground floor store, a partial balcony and the basement.

The owner of the building had come to them with an offer to sell them the building, which was 6 stories high, as he wanted to retire. I think the asking price was about $30,000. Keep in mind that this was in the late 1950s. My idiot clients, who were not very young themselves at this point, turned down the chance to own the building.

One day while I was working with Yetta, the bookkeeper, a disheveled young lady, looking like a mess, came into the store and spoke to Harold. When she was gone, I asked Harold who was this odd looking creature. He told me that she was the president of the cooperative that owned the building and was asking for the rent check. The building that they could have owned for peanuts had been sold for a fortune as each floor was made into spacious apartments.

Neither Harold nor Julius had any children. I know that Harold lived with a woman. He might have been a widower at that point and since they had no one to leave the business to after they were gone, they attempted to sell the business, but it was so specialized and required so much knowledge of the machinery involved that no one came along to buy the business. They had an auction of the inventory and they did quite well with that. I acquired an antique wooden chest containing about 20 drawers that were designed to hold small parts. I refinished it and have it sitting in my office.

Since the business was not too far from Chinatown, Harold would take Fred and me there for lunch at his favorite restaurant. He was a fine fellow. They had one other brother whom I met when he was visiting them. He lived in Los Vegas and said that he had the largest pawnshop in Vegas. Who am I to argue?

My Boyhood Friend's Brother Becomes A Client.

One of my boyhood friends was Jacob Jacobson, known as "Curby". He acquired the name because of his proficiency in playing curb ball. For those of you not old enough to know the game, and I am certain you are in the majority, curb ball was played in the gutters of New York. The curbs of the sidewalks at that time had a rounded metal rim at the top of the curb. The player would throw his ball at the curb, hoping to hit the metal rim. The ball hopefully would fly across the gutter to the other side of the street. The player would run across the street to first base, second base and back home again, unless the ball had been caught on the fly or the player tagged out. The field was an equilateral triangle with home plate being at the apex or curb area.

Curby had an older brother, Merkey. Do not ask me where that name came from. Merkey was unlucky enough to have been born in the wrong year. He was caught in the first draft and spent a year in the army. He was not out very long, when the Second World War came along and back he went into the army. They shipped him off to Africa. He survived and spent more than five years in service.

When he got out, he went into the office supply business in New Jersey. I began doing his accounting. He was kind of the forerunner of Staples. He bought a truck and delivered all the office supplies from his inventory to his customers. It was rough going at the beginning, but slowly he built up his customer base and expanded his business. The sales each month continued to increase. He had a pleasant personality and serviced his customers.

Merkey got married. I met his wife and although she did not help him in his business, she was in the store quite often. After a few months, she approached me while Merkey was out making deliveries. She asked me when I thought Merkey would be ready to file for bankruptcy. I asked her what she was talking about since business was coming along nicely She told me that her father had filed for bankruptcy three times and walked away each time with a great deal of money.

Truthfully, I had no idea how to respond to this character. When Merkey returned I told him what his wife had said and he already knew about her scheme. She must have worked on him, because a few months later I was replaced. I can only guess her father's criminal accountant replaced me.

I heard from Curby months later that Merkey was out of business and divorced.

Amy's Friend's Parents Become Clients.

My middle daughter, Amy had a school friend named Nan. They were very close and we got to meet and socialize with her parents. They were lovely people and we became good friends with Norman and Beverly Weitman. He was a top executive with Paramount Pictures. His family had been very important people in the movie industry for many years and his last name was very well known. I believe he had decision-making authority to decide which motion pictures Paramount would produce.

Norman was a large man. One Saturday night we all went to dinner at the North Shore Steak House, where he was well known. He was not wearing a jacket and the Maitre D insisted that he put on a brown cotton jacket that they supplied him. It was sizes too small and made him look ridiculous. After we were seated he discarded the jacket. Then they seated us at a table under a leaking pipe that dripped water on his head. We changed tables. After we had finished our dinner, he requested that the steak his wife had not finished eating be packed up for him to take home. The piece de resistance was when they brought the piece of steak in a clear plastic bag. He went ballistic and rightfully so.

They lived in a magnificent home in Kings Point. The basement was a fully equipped movie theatre and we enjoyed many evenings watching movies that had not been released as yet.

Norman was a dark swarthy individual. He spoke to me one day and asked me for some accounting and estate planning advice. He then asked if I would prepare his tax returns in the future. Obviously I accepted.

Norman had a dark spot on his forearm that most unfortunately turned into a melanoma. By the time they discovered the melanoma it had already spread throughout his body and he knew he was dying. He never told me that he knew he was dying but in the planning we both did for his estate, it was obvious to me that he was aware that he did not have long to live.

He died shortly thereafter and I handled his estate and personal tax returns. His widow and I went to the New York office of Paramount Pictures. She and I were greeted by many of the top executives and we sat down in a conference room with two of the executives. They were most gracious in giving the widow the Lincoln automobile that he had been driving and as many pension and other benefits that they could conceive. They even offered her a job with the company.

My wife and Beverly remained close and we did what we could to comfort her. Once again, tragedy struck and Beverly was discovered to have Hodgkin's disease. She struggled with it for months. We feel she was not properly taken care of by her doctors, because our oldest daughter had been cured from the same ailment.

Before she died, she appointed me trustee of the funds she would be leaving to her two daughters. She wanted me to keep all the funds in trust for five years before distributing the principal to the girls. Her husband had always provided for her and she had never been required to work. Nan was married and her husband insisted that she work to share their financial burdens and that upset Beverly. She was afraid of what would happen if he and Nan suddenly came into a huge sum of money.

Beverly passed away and once again I prepared the estate and income tax returns. I had control of the funds and the daughters could not draw any money without my consent. Nan, at this point was an attorney. I spoke to her on the phone and told her that we must fund the trusts for five years, in accordance with her mother's wishes. She refused to sign the necessary papers to fund the trusts and said she wanted all of her money now. I told her that I had promised her mother to hold onto the funds for the five-year period.

I had not requested any fees for being the trustee. Nan served me with a summons demanding that I resign as trustee. I spoke to Irving G. an attorney client of mine. He advised me to forget the whole thing and resign. I could not do that and still live with myself.

I gave Irving a check for $1,500 to represent me in this matter. We went to court and I was placed on the witness stand. Nan was represented by another attorney from the firm where she was employed. He questioned me intensely and I explained to him and the judge the entire story of the father and mother's wishes and my moral obligation to fulfill them. Of course, the judge reserved decision and we were told he would render his verdict in due course.

As I was leaving the courtroom, Nan's attorney spoke to me. He told me that he believed my entire testimony. He said that Nan had told him that I was an ogre and a terrible person. He also said that he would no longer represent Nan. The judge ruled in my favor. By this time more than two years had elapsed since the death of Beverly, I had been vindicated in the courtroom and I no longer had the stomach to continue this disagreeable situation. I resigned as trustee and turned the funds over to the two daughters.

My Jailbird Clients

I have intentionally changed the names of the people I am about to describe to protect their families. These people were sent to jail but have since been released.

Two brothers owned another of the large clients that I worked at while I was still an employee. It was a textile firm. The brothers usually fought with each other but they were quite successful. George was their top salesman and I became friendly with him. He asked me to prepare his tax return. I went to his apartment, which was on 90th Street and Broadway. It was a huge apartment with a mammoth living room, dining room and kitchen. I usually did not like going to people's home to gather their information. But, in this case it was a sheer delight. He and his wife were born in Hungary and she was a super cook and baker. We had a huge delicious dinner every time. George and Betty his wife had three children, two boys and one girl. George liked to gamble and enjoyed his card games. He was also very charitable. He could not refuse any request from any Jewish organization.

After we finished dinner, George brought out his twelve monthly bank statements with all the cancelled checks. He and I sorted the contribution checks in piles placing all the $5, $10, $18, and $36 and so forth in separate piles. There were literally hundreds of checks. George and his wife wanted to move to California to join friends and relatives who had already moved there, but they were waiting for the owner of the building in which they lived to co-op the building. They hoped they would buy their apartment and then sell it a substantial profit. Well, they waited and they waited but it never happened. So, they just gave up and moved. The Oriental rug that they had in their living was huge and brought them I think $24,000.

Marvin and Steward their two sons stayed in touch with me. Marvin went into business with Michael, a friend. They went into the office equipment supply business and eventually obtained a major office copier manufacturer as a supplier. They opened their business in New Jersey. I became their accountant and worked closely with them as their accountant and mentor. Marvin and I went out to California to look at a computer system that he purchased and installed. It was a completely comprehensive system tracking receivables, payables and inventory. I felt very close to these two men. Fred, I, Michael and a friend of his went to Canada fishing twice and had a grand time.

Steward, Marvin's brother had gone into the restaurant business with a friend of his. I did not become his accountant immediately. They had another accountant and after a while they became unhappy with him and engaged me. The restaurant was located just opposite the United Nations. Their landlord was the United Nations Foundation. It was a magnificent restaurant and became quite well known. My daughter Amy was married there in the spring of 1981 and it was a lovely affair.

In spite of its popularity, the restaurant never seemed to do very well. They paid a monthly basic rent and an additional rent predicated on their sales over a specified amount. I had to prepare the statements to be presented to the landlord. Many is the month when I had to skip being paid because they would tell me that I could see that things were not going well and I would have to wait.

After a few years, a legitimate business broker approached them. The broker had called them and asked if the restaurant was for sale? Well, obviously everything is for sale if the price is tempting. The broker showed up with two well-dressed gentlemen and negotiations were begun. Of course the owners presented to the potential buyers my financial reports. They looked at the reports and must have said that there is no way that the restaurant was worth the price that they were asking I am assuming that the two "potential" buyers then began the "good guy bad guy routine". The "bad guy" must have asked to see the "real" set of books and the "good guy" must have said that they had no right to ask that. I was not present at this meeting, thank goodness. My clients must have brought out their "private records" to show the potential buyers. The broker and the potential buyers must have said that they would think about it and get back to my clients.

Seven AM the next morning, police, FBI agents and IRA agents surrounded the restaurant. They went into the restaurant and removed every piece of paper they could find. All the bookkeeping records, legitimate, illegal and all the paper towels, toilet tissue and you name it. I heard about the raid soon after it took place.

I was working in my office some days after the raid, when two men walked in. Both were at least six feet tall, weighing about 170 pounds each and both wearing brown raincoats. I turned to them and said, "FBI". They said, "How did you know?" I was handed a summons to appear before a grand jury.

Fortunately for me, my oldest daughter, Susan, is an attorney. She was a partner in a large law firm. One of the partners was Mr. Armstrong. He was the attorney who was involved in the Knapp Commission in New York City. Susan arranged an appointment for me to see Mr. Armstrong. When I went in to see him, he called the District Attorney and spoke with him. He told the District Attorney that I was the father of one of his partners and wanted to know what they wanted of me. The District Attorney told him that he knew that I was not part of the conspiracy and they just wanted me to verify the records they had taken from the premise.

When I went to the grand jury, I was asked to identify the books and records that I had worked on. They showed me other journals that I had never seen and I told them so. They wanted to know if I had socialized with the owners and had I even been to their apartments. The answer was no in both cases.

Fortunately I could tell the truth because I had not been to their apartments and had never socialized with either of them. I knew that Stewart's apartment had been photographed and written up in a magazine, but he had not let them use his name or his address, which made sense.

It turned out that the FBI caught the company from whom they purchased their meat. The meat dealer sang a tune and named all of their customers who were paying them in cash. Somehow, my clients had opened bank accounts in Philadelphia and were able to deposit some of the American Express charges there. I cannot imagine how they went about it but they did. I have no idea how much they had skimmed in all the years they had been in business. Of course those bank accounts did not appear on the books and those were the funds they skimmed plus I assume all or most of the cash that customers paid.

Not only did they cheat the IRS but they also cheated their landlord. They both went to jail in sequence so that they could continue their business. Needless to say, I immediately dropped them as a client. A few weeks later I got another visit from the FBI and they had some more questions. I told them that I no longer represented them The FBI man said, 'we did not tell you to give them up as a client." I told him to get lost. They went out of business shortly thereafter. I am sure the landlord refused to renew their lease.

It was a pity and just stupidity on their part. They killed the goose that was laying a nice golden egg for them, but greed did them in. They probably laughed themselves silly at the end of each of my visits. I would tell them how little profit they showed that month or the amount of loss and then they must have then gone to their private records and combined that with my figures to obtain the real profit for the previous month.

Now For The Kick In The Backside.

I continued on as the accountant for Marvin. He joined an organization of young successful executives and became enthralled with his membership. He was not happy that I had dropped his brother and I tried to explain to him my position and that I had little choice in not remaining the accountant for the restaurant. Marvin called me one day and told me that he was changing accountants. He had met another accountant who would steer him into profitable investments. To say that I was upset would be putting it mildly. I had gone out of my way to help him and his partner grow. I met the new accountant and turned over my records to him. A phony of the first order. He was in the business of selling tax shelters and of course he got Marvin and Michael to make investments in which they would receive documentation from partnerships to deduct losses on their tax returns of four or five times their investments. In subsequent years the Internal Revenue Service jumped on these illegal transactions and recouped the taxes the participants had wrongfully deducted on their tax returns. I can only hope that Marvin got his comeuppance.

More Jailbirds

Marvin and his partner were not the only jailbirds that I had as clients. Back to Wasserman and Taten for this next episode. One of their clients was a lovely man named Abe. He owned a business called Abe's Auto Sets, Inc. For those of you not old enough to remember automobile seat covers let me explain that automobile owners would purchase plastic covers for the seats in their cars to preserve them and keep them clean. Abe made seat covers for every car in existence at that time. He kind of got fed up paying large accounting fees and when he heard that I had gone into business for myself, he contacted me. He was the only one of Wasserman and Taten clients that I got directly from them, of course other than Nat Sheinman. Over and above making seat covers, he tried his hand at some other products, using the same materials that he used for the seat covers. One item was a blanket for use at outdoors-cold weather sports such as football and soccer. The blanket came inside a case made from the auto seat cover material.

At that time there was an 8% federal excise tax on auto accessories. Abe's business began to fade as less and less people purchased auto seat covers. He fell behind in paying the federal excise tax. Since the excise tax had been collected from his customers they were deemed to be trust funds, just the same as sales tax is considered. Since they were trust funds, it would not have helped Abe to file for bankruptcy because it would not have absolved him from the liability to the Internal Revenue Service. I suggested to Abe that we do something, which would be very unorthodox but might work. I arranged a date with the Internal Revenue Service with Abe to discuss his problem. I explained to the IRS that Sam owed the money and wanted to do everything he could to assist the IRS in collecting the money due to them. I told the representative of the IRS that Sam had substantial inventory of finished products and he was willing to turn his inventory over to the government and have them hold an auction and probably receive all the monies due to them. There would be no funds left for any other creditor but Abe could walk away unencumbered. The IRS representative said he had never heard anything like this but he would discuss it with his superiors. They accepted my cockeyed idea and sent a crew of IRS employees to Abe's place of business to take an inventory and arrange for the sale. The IRS employees got filthy and hated what they had to do, but the auction took place. All of Abe's customers and others attended and bought the seat covers. The IRS, as I predicted, raised enough funds to cover Abe's liability and he retired without a cloud hanging over his head.

Abe's son Bill had worked for his father selling the auto seat covers. His customers were new and used car dealers. The phrase "previously owned or pre owned" had not been invented yet. When Abe went out of business his son had to do something to earn a living. He had made enough connections in the industry to open his own used car business on Jerome Avenue in the Bronx. If you are familiar with the Bronx then you know that Jerome Avenue was the Mecca for the used car business. There were many used car dealers there and even though they sold used cars to the public, the backbone of their business were sales to other retail used car dealers. Bill made connections with the large car rental and leasing companies and purchased cars coming off lease and cars from the rental companies in great quantities.

The car rental companies would sell their cars after a short period of ownership. Some of the cars would be sold at auctions. He would attempt to negotiate the price that he paid for the cars after he had already sold them to insure that he made a profit. He knew how to negotiate and deal with his suppliers.

Over and above selling his cars domestically, Murray developed a business of selling his cars to overseas customers. Bill had Sal as a partner. Sal had his own list of customers. They had a salesman who would travel to Europe to arrange for the sale of cars.

I enjoyed having them as a client and benefited greatly by having the opportunity to buy good used cars inexpensively. I used to change cars every few months. After I had a car for a while, Bill would tell me to bring it back as he had a customer for the car and for me to take another auto.

The used car industry in the 1950 and 1960 was completely different than what exists today. There was a man, known on Jerome Avenue as Max the Clock. Max walked up and down Jerome Avenue wheeling his toolbox on a length of metal pipe. For $10 or $20 Max would move one of the cars to edge of the lot. He would get under the car with his "tools" and within 10 minutes the odometer in the car was reduced from fifty or sixty thousands miles to ten to twenty thousand miles. It was prevalent on the "street". Eventually the federal government made it a federal crime to change the mileage on autos.

The FBI must have become aware of Max the Clock and the story goes that they followed him and videotaped him performing his miracles. Max was arrested and he sang like a canary. The first of the used car dealers, who was arrested, threw himself on the mercy of the court and pleaded guilty. He received a $100,000 fine and must have been warned against continuing the practice. Max the Clock disappeared from the face of the earth.

Bill and Sal were indicted for changing the mileage of their autos. I suggested to Bill to plead guilty and hope for the best. Bill was one of the most stubborn individuals you could encounter. He hired an attorney. The attorney told him that he would get Bill off the hook on a technicality. Bill contended that the only cars, on which he changed the odometers, were those cars that he shipped overseas and therefore the United States Government had no jurisdiction. After the attorney received $100,000 in fees, he came to Bill and suggested that he accept a guilty plea. Bill went ballistic, fired the attorney and hired another. Well after three more attorneys and another $300,000 down the tubes, Bill and Sal were brought to court.

I was home with the flu when Bill's trial began. He begged me to come to court as a character witness. I had known him for so many years that I could not refuse to do as he asked. He sent a driver and a car for me. The judge was an African American woman named Constance Baker Motley. I was placed on the witness stand, along with Bill's rabbi and other character witnesses. I told how many years I have known him and his family and what a wonderful husband and father he was. It was a complete waste of my time. In effect, the judge said "do not try to confuse me with the facts because my mind's made up." Bill and Sal were read the riot act and were sentenced to a year and one half each. They went to a minimum-security prison in Pennsylvania. Sal was working in the library, I did not know he could read, and he fell off a ladder and broke his leg. Bill engaged at the end a famous criminal lawyer, Barry Slotnick, who got their sentences reduced to one year. They got out of jail and had to spend some time at a half way house until they were finally released. Bill before he went to jail had been a strong, aggressive, self-important individual. When he came out he was a shadow of his former self and never really recovered from his jail experience.

Bill moved to Florida and went into the used car business with his younger son. We remained his accountants and my partner Fred, whose parents were now living in Florida, would go down quarterly. Bill died from cancer recently and his son tried to hold on to the business but it failed and they closed the business.

As a result of the trials and tribulations that Bill and Sal went through, the Internal Revenue must have gotten wind of the case against them. The Internal Revenue came to call. The agent came in with a chip on his shoulder and felt certain that he would end up with a sizeable assessment. In spite of the trouble that they had gotten themselves into, the books of the corporation were clean. After much feuding and discussion, the agent finally conceded that even though the owners were about to become jailbirds there were no additional taxes due.

While still in business Bill and Sal had taken in a third partner, whose name escapes me at the moment. A stockholder's agreement was drawn and they decided to take out $250,000 life insurance on each of the stockholders. They all passed the physical exam with flying colors. Unfortunately, the newest member very shortly afterwards developed lung cancer. He died soon after the disease was discovered. A claim was filed with the two life insurance companies who had issued the policies. One of the companies paid the beneficiary, the brother of the deceased, almost immediately. The other company stalled with the payment. The agent who sold them the policies came to visit and said something like "you know he did not pay premiums very long." Bill almost twisted his neck. The company did make the other payment and then the brother came to collect the proceeds. He then made some small talk and got around to saying that now that he had collected the insurance, he wanted to be paid for his brother's one-third interest in the corporation. I brought out the stockholder's agreement and showed him the paragraph that spelled out what happens in the event of death. The beneficiary would receive the insurance proceeds or one-third the book value of the corporation, which ever was higher but would not be entitled to both. The brother went home with his tail dragging between his legs but richer by a quarter of a million dollars.

Now I Become The Accountant For A New Car

Dealer.

One of Bill's customers was Ruby Schneier. He bought used cars for new car dealers who wanted to increase their inventory of pre owned cars. I saw Ruby quite often and always had an interesting conversation with him. I started to prepare his tax returns. Ruby then had an opportunity to purchase a fifty-percent interest in a Lincoln Mercury dealer in Nassau County. I went to review the books for Ruby and helped him work out a reasonable purchase agreement. His partner was not overly in love with his present accountant and apparently realized what a good job I had done for Ruby in representing him in the purchase of his interest. So, I became their accountant and had to get a complete new accounting education. The bookkeeping system for a new car dealer is very complex. A good bookkeeper at a new car dealer is worth her weight in new cars. The manufacturers want a monthly detailed report spelling out the income and expenses of each department at the dealer. After a while I got the system under my belt and things went along smoothly. The auto companies send in their auditors periodically to check up on the dealers. They usually show up unannounced. The biggest concern that the dealer has is to be out of "trust". This means that the dealer would have sold a car, delivered it to the customer and had gotten paid for the car, but had not have made payment to the auto company timely.

If a car dealer were to show you the invoice from the car manufacturer to impress you with how little profit they are making on the car that they are selling you. Forget it. That invoice doesn't begin to tell the whole story. There are all sorts of rebates, discounts and advertising allowances that come to the car dealer.

Ruby's partner came from a rather wealthy family. They had made their fortune in feathers. The partner decided that he wanted to retire and I think he wanted to move to Florida. Again, Ruby and I worked out a buyout of the partner and Ruby became the sole owner. His son, Steve, came to work in the showroom. The business did well, mainly because Ruby knew how to sell individual buyers and sales of Lincoln Town Car fleets. With Murray out of business in New York, at this point, I began to purchase my cars from Ruby. I drove Lincoln town cars for years and loved them.

Ruby developed a serious heart condition and needed an operation. However, his condition was so dire; no local cardiologist would venture to perform the operation because they could not guarantee his survival. Someone put him in touch with a cardiac specialist out west. He sent his records out there and was advised that they thought they could help him. He went there, they operated and he survived and recovered. Ruby was a sailor and always owned large powerboats. He loved playing the role of Captain. His wife hated it and did not like keeping the boat spic and span. They began to separate and were heading for divorce. I am sad to say that they never got divorced because she became quite ill and died.

Ruby was a dandy and quite vain. He had developed carbuncles on both of his elbows. He was warned by his cardiologist not have them removed by an operation because it would be too dangerous for his health and heart condition. He had acquired a girl friend by this time. Foolishly, he ignored the advice of his doctors and went ahead with the operation. The predictions unfortunately were very accurate and Ruby went into shock on the operating table, or whatever happened, but he became a vegetable. He ended up in a nursing home and his son visited him every day. Ruby lasted for months in a fetal position, but eventually succumbed.

Steve took over the business but he had not acquired from his father the talent he needed to succeed. He poured a fortune into the business desperately hoping to keep it afloat He brought in Porsches, jet skis and tried everything he could think of but unfortunately after about two years, he had to close his doors.

He now works as a salesman selling Rolls Royce, Bentleys, Porsches, etc and is still a client.

I Receive An Opportunity To Expand My Practice.

One day while working at a client, I received a call from the controller who worked for Nat Sheinman. He told me that a friend of his had died and his widow wanted to sell his accounting practice. This must have been around 1955. I contacted the widow and negotiated with her to purchase the practice. It was an odd practice. It included several small ladies department stores in State College, Pa, Johnstown, Pa and Butler, Pa. These stores would forward the invoices they received for the merchandise they purchased to the accounting office. The ladies in the accounting office would enter the invoice in a purchase journal and voucher them for payment after deducting the trade discount. They would mail the vouchers back to the client for payment. I spoke with the clients in Johnstown and Butler and they agreed to us continuing on to work for them. The client from State College, Mr. Charles Schlow somehow found my telephone number at home on my unlimited local phone. We had quite a conversation and when all was said and done, Mr. Schlow said I sounded like a nice "hamish" boy (Yiddush for someone who is down to earth and can be trusted) and I can come out to State College to work for them.

For me, it was a dream come true. I had been stationed at State College, PA, the home of Penn State University from June 1943 to March 1944 as I have described previously. I had loved it there and going back was something to which I looked forward, Mr. Schlow was an unusual individual and quite brilliant. Like many Jewish men who had come from Europe at an early stage of their lives, he must have started out as a humble peddler in Bellefonte, PA. From those beginnings he opened up a ladies department store first in a smaller town outside of State College and then on the main street in State College known as East College Avenue. Over and above the ladies shop, he had a furniture store and a movie house. Not too many of you will remember a silent movie actress by the name of Helen Twelvetrees. The movies house was called Twelvetrees and showed mostly arty films

Mr. Schlow's daughter Irma and son in law Harold Zipser ran the dress shop, His son Frank managed the furniture store and the movie house just ran on its own. Harold had been a podiatrist and had moved to State College and opened a practice. He met Irma Zipser and they married and had two daughters, Judith and Ruth. Mr. Schlow must have talked Harold into selling his practice and join the family business. No grass grew under Charles' feet; he owned the building that housed the store, which contained several apartments on the second level and the company offices. He built two other apartment houses.

Mr. Schlow was a widower and I arrived on the scene after his wife Bella had died. He single-handedly financed and built a library in town. The library has since been rebuilt but still retains the name of the Bella Schlow Memorial Library. There was some talk about changing the name, but that was short lived. He lived in a lovely home and owned land adjacent to his house, which was the size of a city block. He allowed his neighbors to have garden plots on the land, which I am sure they enjoyed.

Charles had a library of hundreds of books, many of them first editions. I asked him one day if he had read all of these books and he replied, "Some of them twice." He appointed himself unofficial rabbi in the local prison that housed some Jewish prisoners. He would visit them every Jewish holiday and bring them food, wine and some solace. He had a great sense of humor. He told me a story about one of his visits to the penitentiary. He had decided one Friday to visit with his "congregation". He always had to call ahead to the warden whenever he wanted to visit. The warden told him that he did not know of any Jewish holiday that weekend. Charles replied, "Oh it is erev shabbas", which means it is the evening before the Sabbath.

One winter visit I ended up with Charles' overcoat and ended up taking it in error back to New York. We were about the same size and it really was funny. Sometimes I would fly to State College, which was quite difficult. You would fly non-stop to Pittsburgh and then take a very small plane back to Black Moshannon Forest airport. It was a tiny airport with a tin shack for a terminal. Someone had to drive out to the runway to chase away the deer before a plane could land. I had all sort of experiences trying to get there especially in bad weather. The pilot tried landing one time and had to abort the landing because of the deep snow on the runway and we went on to DuBois, about a hundred miles away. They drove us back to State College on an icy trip. I arrived in town at 5 PM just about time to quit working for the day.

One of the times that I drove in the winter, the snow was falling heavily and so deep that I had to follow in the tracks of a tractor-trailer that was just ahead of me. I arrived safely but while working at the store the next day, a salesman came in to see Harold and told us that he was about an hour behind me the day before and the state police forced him off Route 80 and made him check into a motel.

Sometimes I would take a bus to Lewistown and then the Penn Railroad to New York. That was the way I would go home weekends when I was stationed there. This one time Charles stayed with me while

I waited for the bus. We had lots of time and went in the coffee shop for a cup of coffee and a piece of pie. While there Charles struck up a conversation with a nice looking lady. My bus came along and I was gone. When I got back three months later, Irma told me that Mr. Schlow was now dating this lady.

He eventually met a lady from New York and married her. She came to live in State College but did not care for it and was really a New York City lady. She came to me one day complaining that she just found out that Mr. Schlow was ten years older than he had told her. It should not have bothered her, because soon after they wed, she became ill and passed away. Her daughter came visiting looking for some type of inheritance and she was sent on her way.

Frank Schlow sadly developed Hodgkin's disease in an advanced stage. He knew he would not last very long. He and his wife Martie went on an extended cruise to enjoy what little time they had left. After he passed away they closed the furniture store.

Penn State has many professors who are quite brilliant. They start up engineering and other companies. The Weather Channel was founded at Penn State and still exists there. Charles having taught a little at Penn State knew many of the staff. He was getting ready to go on a vacation when he was approached to purchase some stock in a fledgling company. He gave $10,000 to his son Frank and told him to purchase stock in the new company. Frank bought the stock and they issued the stock in his name. When Frank passed away Charles told Martie, Frank's widow, that the stock in Frank's name was really his stock. By this time the stock had doubled in value and was worth $20,000. Foolishly Martie told Charles that she does not know anything about the stock transaction and she deemed the stock to be her inheritance. Charles was not one to quibble and wrote Martie a check for $20,000 and took the stock. What the silly woman did cost her and her family a fortune. Charles immediately rewrote his will and cut her and her three children out of their inheritance.

I have become extremely friendly with the Schlow and Zipser families. Charles died well into his nineties. He once told me that he was very lonely. I suggested he call some of his friends. He said, "I can't, they are all dead." Harold and Irma decided to close the department store and rent it out for the income. So, they then became only a real estate company with at least 100 apartments that they rented to undergraduates and graduate students. Running the real estate business became the job of Harold and his son in law Peter Lang. Peter had married Judith and they had two daughters.

Harold developed emphysema and had to have a supply of oxygen handy at all times. He lived with the malady for quite a while but it finally got the better of him and he passed away. His son in law was an extremely obese individual and Harold asked him many times, "how many people do you see who are 65 years old and your size?" Peter ran the real estate business sitting in the office and was not able to go to the buildings to check up on them and their state of condition.

Harold's predication came true and unfortunately Peter died at an early age. Irma and her two daughters could not, nor did they want to run the real estate business. While Peter and Harold ran the business they had two men working for them full time taking care of the buildings and a bookkeeper. They owned a truck and had many other expenses. I went to State College and went with the ladies to two different real estate management companies. We were not happy with the first people we met and settled on the second one. They wanted 6% of the gross rent plus $150 for every apartment they rented. Well, these apartments are turned over quite often because of the type of tenants and the $150 would have added up to a substantial sum. I made a counter proposal that my client would pay 6 and ½% in lieu of the $150 for renting to new tenants. They thought I was nuts and they did not know how they could refigure their computer program for the different rate. I told them it was their problem and they would work it out. They did.

The Real Estate Management Company mails to my office every month a detailed list of all the rent they have collected and the funds they have expended on behalf of the client. I have asked them to supply me with additional information from time to time relative to seeing receipts for their expenditures. They come with silly reasons why they cannot or will not reply to my requests. Irma's daughters have written to me telling me to stop harassing the real estate company and that they are happy with what is being done. Needless to say, I have placed the daughters' letter in a safe place for future reference if I ever need it.

The kickbacks and the over rides that are being received by the real estate Management Company are shameful. I was interested in safeguarding my position as auditor. A neighbor of mine who is an accountant was sued by a client. It was the same type of arrangement that I have, except it was not done by mail but by actually visiting the client's office. In that instance, the real estate management firm said they were paying the real estate taxes and the suppliers but they were not The accountants lost the case, must have had a substantial payment to make, and nearly had to go out of business because of their neglect.

Ruth Zipser married the father of the men who are running the restaurant that they rent from the Zipsers. We are not doing the tax returns for the daughters. Peter had some other business dealings in State College and used a local accountant to prepare his returns and Ruth is now using her husband's accountant. I continue to prepare the trust and personal tax returns for their mother Irma.

We Purchase Another Accounting Practice

We had rented a room in our suite to a lovely man. His name was Sam Samuels and he was also a CPA. He was with us for quite a while and we got along famously. He was just a decent individual. One day he went to work in Manhattan. His wife waited for him at the Long Island railroad station in Roslyn. The train was very late in arriving and Ruth, his wife, overheard some of the passenger as they got off the train, say that they were delayed because some poor soul had died of a heart attack in Penn Station. Unfortunately, the man who died was Sam Samuels. We bought his few clients from the wife and arranged a pay out of five years.

One of the clients we purchased was a team of obstetricians. We remained their accountants for the five years of the payout and then were told that they are changing accountants. Not that they were dissatisfied with our service, but they owed their business to another friend. They had promised Ruth that they would stay with us as long as we were paying for their business. She must have told them that the purchase price would be adjusted downward if we lost any of the clients during the five years.

We purchased and retained as a client a cousin of Sam Samuels. His name was Harry Samuels. Harry was quite an individual. He made his fortune by arranging the sales or mergers of large corporations. He had an office in Nassau County where he read and studied hundreds of annual financial reports of public companies. His reputation preceded him. He had entrée into many of the major corporations and was written up on the front page of the business section of the New York Times. Once he located a company that he thought might be available to purchase or merge with another company, or one that might be interested in selling their business, he would contact them. If they were interested, he would get them to sign an iron bound contract authorizing his to negotiate a sale or merger for which he would receive 5% of the proceeds. He successfully consummated many deals. He told me that almost invariably after the deals were consummated and he applied for his fee, he would be told something like, "Harry, what did you do? You made a few telephone calls and how can you really expect to paid some a large sum for your endeavors?" His response was "you will hear from my attorney in the morning." He received his fees and sometimes took stock as part of his fee.

Harry and his wife Ruth had three sons. A twin and a younger son. One of the twins followed in his father's footsteps when Harry died and also became very successful. Unfortunately he died at very young age.

The youngest son, Jonathan, became a doctor and is still a client of mine. Jonathan is extremely bright and in addition to seeing patients he is the executive director of a hospital. His wife is also a doctor.

Another of the clients we purchased was a very interesting client and the gentleman who owned the business was interesting as well. His name was Sam Sall. Sam had graduated as an attorney in the height of the big depression and could not find a job. He gave up trying to become a lawyer and went to work for a company that manufactured toilet paper, facial tissue, paper napkins and other paper products. He became a top-notch salesman and eventually acquired the company when the owner retired or passed away. They sold their products to the finest department stores in this country. Sam had designers working for him who designed the boxes and wrappers in accordance with the wishes and approval of the customers. The term "private label" was the appropriate designation for what Sam accomplished. He knew how to wine, dine and entertain his customers, send them wonderful gifts and retained their loyalty and their business.

Sam could be the kindest gentlest man anyone would want to know and then turn around and become nasty, vicious and mean. The company consisted of three people, Sam, Sol, his brother and Sarah,

Sol's wife. Sarah was an excellent bookkeeper, secretary and Sol ran the technical end of the business processing the orders, tending to the billing and collecting. They had no manufacturing facilities at all and operated from a small office. When I first went to work with them, they were in the Flatiron district in New York and then moved their office to Long Beach. Sam lived in a cooperative apartment in Long Beach so it became convenient for him to be there.

Sol would process the orders received by Sam by buying the merchandise from the giant producers of the items they needed. They bought from Kleenex, Kimberly Clark, Marcal and others. They would hide the fact that they did not have any factory by having their suppliers deliver the products in tractor-trailers. They would place a magnetic placard on the cab of the tractors bearing the name of "House Products Inc" which of course was the name of Sam's company. On rare occasions Marcal or one of the other suppliers would neglect to put the placard in place. Sam would get a call from his customer wanting to know what was going on. Sam would tell them that he was so busy and short of mobile equipment and had to borrow the tractor from his competitor. I overheard him telling the story and he got away with it.

Sam was in a good mood one day and bought Sarah a brand new car. Sol was a real character and would never her drive the car. Only after Sol died did Sarah get to drive. But I was witness to Sam in a foul mood when he would scream at Sarah for some silly little thing she did wrong. Sol used to come to me continually and tell me that he could no longer take the abuse and had to quit. My advice was always the same. I told Sol that his brother could not last much longer and he stood to inherit at least two million dollars and for that kind of money he should be able to cope with Sam's outbursts.

One year I raised Sam's fee for the preparation of his tax returns by $100. I thought he was going to have a stroke. He said, "how could I raise the fee without discussing it with him and $100 was entirely too much?" I told him to forget about it and just pay the same fee as the previous year.

Sam had never married and Sol was his only living relative. Sam always had a woman living with him and for a short time he had two women in the apartment. He outlived several women. Every time one of them expired he immediately had the next one move in with him. Sam spent six months each year at his apartment in Bal Harbour, Florida and the ladies were only too happy to enjoy life with Sam. He was wealthy and generous with the ladies. He told me that the only woman he had ever asked to marry him turned him down because her mother had told her that it made no sense marrying a toilet paper salesman. Little did she know? But, that lady was the last one to move in with Sam.

Sam came to me when I was working there one day and asked me to become a joint executor with his brother. He did not trust his brother to take care of the woman, in accordance with the terms of his will. He made me promise to see to it that the woman he was living with would enjoy the use of the apartment in Long Beach and the apartment in Florida at no expense to her. I took it very seriously and I did promise Sam to fulfill his wishes. He changed his will and made me a co-executor. When Sam passed away I received an executor commission of $68,000. If Sam knew that I received that sum he would come back from the grave. I followed his wishes and Sol did not complain. The woman only lasted about six months after Sam died. Sol tried continuing the business but the suppliers, basically Marcal, saw an opportunity to take over Sam's customers. They knew who the customers were, because they were delivering to them. Marcal told Sol that they would no longer process his orders and he had no choice but to close the doors

We Keep Moving On and Up

Jack Goldman was another of my clients. He manufactured storm windows and storm doors and operated first in Queens and then in Copiague Long Island. He was reasonably successful and sold to contractors, do it yourselfers and installers. I wrote to the New York State Sales Tax Commission and detailed all the various aspects of this business. I asked them to advise me as to when sales tax should or need not be charged to the customers. In their brilliance they replied and told us to do whatever we wished and if it was wrong they would tell us at the time on an examination. Some of his customers were policeman, firemen and others who would moonlight doing installations in their spare time to earn some additional funds. One of the policemen, Conrad Miller was a good customer. Jack and Conrad had many things in common and were both pilots. Jack and Dorothy, his wife, decided to retire and move to Florida. Conrad was leaving or had already left the Nassau Police Department and offered to buy the business. They negotiated a price and Conrad and his brother took over the business. I think his brother had worked at Grumman as an engineer. I knew he was building an airplane in his basement.

Conrad retained me as his accountant and I have been his confidant, friend and accountant for many years up until today. Conrad is a most unusual individual. He has little understanding of a financial statement and as many times as I have tried to teach him how to decipher a balance sheet and a profit and loss statement, he just does not get it. If the balance sheet has an "Earned Surplus" figure of $50,000, Conrad will scream at me that he did not make $50,000 last month or last year. I have to explain that the "Earned Surplus" is the accumulation of all the net profits from all the years he has been in business.

However, Conrad, who has no formal engineering education, can and has taken apart every machine in the factory, repaired it and put it back together in perfect working order.

Conrad divorced his wife and married a lovely woman named Joan. Joan Miller came from a family who owned funeral homes and it was her function to dress and apply makeup to the deceased. She is a horsewoman. She and Conrad visited some friends in Virginia, fell in love with the country and she bought a farm with hundreds of acres in Warrenton, Virginia.

Conrad sold the business to some shady characters, who eventually paid him all they owed him, but it took some doing on Conrad's part to collect. You do not want to owe money to Conrad and not pay.

Conrad went into retirement for a short period but could not take the sedentary life. He opened a small shop to manufacture storm doors and storm windows. He hired a local woman CPA who drove him crazy. She knew how to send invoices but did not understand the business he was in.

I had spoken to her and explained to her how to estimate the inventory at the end of each month in order to arrive at an intelligent profit and loss statement but to no avail.

I have always made it a practice to learn as much as I can about the clients' business. I always go into the factory or machine shop to learn the details of what is going on, how the products are made and what the costs were to comprise the components.

Conrad knew that I had other clients in Virginia and that he would not have to pay the full fare for me to come to work for him. He called me and we got together again. Joan was now in the horse business and owned boarded and bred thoroughbred horses. She has rarely made money at it, although she would love to make a profit every year. Her horses could have been made into racing horses since they are thoroughbreds. She would not sell her horses for that purpose and only sold them to people to ride, jump and enjoy.

The storm window and storm doors did not go well in Virginia and Conrad got it into his head to go into the tempered glass business. Conrad is a man who once he gets an idea in his head; he moves ahead and gets things done. He bought a piece of land and built a building. To temper glass one has to purchase the machinery at a cost of at least one million dollars. The machinery was purchased from a company in Norway or Finland and they sent a crew to the Virginia to assemble and prepare the machines to function and educate himself and his staff.

Tempering glass is a fascinating process. Obviously car windshields are tempered glass but that is not what Conrad was going to do. Once glass is tempered it cannot be cut, so you had better get it right the first time. Conrad purchased a computing system that calculated the most efficient way to cut the glass, before the tempering process and get the most usable number of pieces from the large sheet of glass. The glass is placed on a wood table. The table has holes in it through which air is blown from underneath so that the sheet can be moved very easily. The sheet of glass, depending on the thickness, can weigh a great deal and would be very difficult to maneuver on the table without the air blowing from underneath. Once the computer has made the calculation, a blade cuts the sheet of glass into the precalculated pieces and a worker then breaks off the excess little pieces. The glass then goes through a washing and drying process and then heads for the oven. The tempering oven can be as long as 50 feet. The glass is heated almost to a molten state and then rapidly cooled. Of course the beauty of tempered glass is that if it breaks it does not break into sharp shards but breaks into small non-injurious pebbles.

My Japanese Connection.

Conrad was growing steadily and although the business was not very profitable, Mitsubishi approached him. They wanted to buy his plant and go into the tempered glass business themselves. I assisted him with the negotiations and at one point Conrad walked out of a meeting fuming. I calmed him down and asked him to let me go back and negotiate on his behalf. He said ok and back we went. We moved on with the negotiations and were scheduled to meet again. I got a call from Mitsubishi and was asked to come to their office in New York City. I went to the meeting that took place in a large conference room. There were about a dozen Japanese men and one Caucasian man. The Japanese each handed me a business card. On one side of the card was their name in Japanese and on the other side was their American name, such as John, Tim, James, etc.

Before the meeting started, I told the group that ethically I could not discuss their pending acquisition. They all agreed that we would not talk about the business in Virginia. They only wanted to know about me, my firm, my experience and so forth. I must have made a decent presentation because they purchased Conrad's business for four million dollars on a Friday. I got a call the following Monday and was asked to go Warrenton on Tuesday to begin working for them.

On my next visit to Warrenton, I had a meeting with Conrad to discuss my fee for the work I had done for him in the negotiations. I told him that I thought what I had accomplished for him was worth $100,000. He went into a rage, yelling and screaming that I was asking way too much. I asked him to sleep on it. I spent the night as usual at his home. We both drove to the factory the next morning. Sometime about mid morning, Conrad invited me into a closet for a private meeting. He told me that he had discussed my request with his wife and had given it some consideration. He then asked me if I would accept $75,000. I agreed graciously and we have still remained very close.

In celebration of Mitsubishi taking over the plant in Warrenton, they had a lovely party. They invited all of the customers, bankers and suppliers. My wife and I attended the party. A top executive from Mitsubishi headquarters attended the party as well. He was a well-groomed, immaculately dressed, handsome man in his 60s. He circulated speaking to many of the guests. Somehow, he hooked on to my wife and spent a great deal of time with her. He wanted to know her opinion of the Japanese and whether she thought they could succeed in Warrenton. My wife gave him her honest thoughts on the subject.

They kept all the American employees and only sent one man from Tokyo to run the business. The Japanese man was called Kiyoshi Matsubara. He worked diligently on his numbers, production and sales records and did everything in his power to make a success of the business. He and I became very close and are still very friendly. He invited me to go to his home for dinner on my next visit. Knowing that Japanese are very big on gifts, I had my wife purchase a lovely piece of glass from Tiffany. I brought it with me on my next visit. Kiyoshi told me that his wife was not ready for that night, so back went the glass with me to New York. The next month the same thing happened again, but on the third visit he took me to his home. I had to remove my shoes and of course I had a hole in my socks.

His wife is a fantastic cook and the meal was absolutely delicious. There was another young Japanese man there for dinner. He spoke English without an accent. He worked for Mitsubishi as did his father and he had lived in the US since childhood. He was soon being transferred to Tokyo and would have to learn to speak Japanese. He and I shared a cab to the motel. I asked the young man if all Japanese women cooked like that. He said, "no way". Kiyoshi's wife, Hisea, was most unusual and a great cook. She had learned her cooking skills from Kiyoshi's mother.

Shortly after dinner, Kiyoshi went upstairs and came down with a Japanese painting. It was very beautiful and was painted by his uncle. It was a still life painting and I admired it and told his so. He said the painting was a gift for me.

I noticed a small grand piano in Kiyoshi's house and asked who played? Kiyoshi told his daughter to play something for me. She sat right down, with no objections, and played beautifully. I can just see an American kid complying with their parent's wishes without grumbling. I asked Kiyoshi if she could be a concert pianist and he said her hands were too small.

Mitsubishi and Kiyoshi tried desperately to succeed but the Virginians would not cooperate. Kiyoshi felt such an attachment to me and had built up such confidence in our relationship that he showed me a confidential map of the United States showing the entire country with concentric circles of tempering plants they planned on owning. For a while I thought Kiyoshi was going to commit hari kari and he did develop high blood pressure. He was failing in his command of the company and was losing money every month.

One night while I was in Warrenton, Kiyoshi's wife was not going to be at home that evening, so Kiyoshi invited me to have dinner with him. Of course I accepted his invitation. We went to a Japanese restaurant in Washington DC. I was the only Caucasian person in the restaurant. All the other patrons were Japanese men. There were no women. Kiyoshi and I sat at the counter and we had our very own cook preparing dishes for us. Naturally Kiyoshi did the ordering and we ate and we ate and we drank Sake and we drank Sake. Kiyoshi got a little drunk and I asked him how he was going to drive home. He said, "You will drive." Kiyoshi could not get over the fact that I knew how to handle chopsticks properly and he asked, "How you know how to do that?" His command of the English language was quite good.

In any event, Mitsubishi decided one day to put the business up for sale. No one offered to buy a business losing money. Mitsubishi had installed additional machinery at a substantial cost to them. They had installed a computer system that would allow them to unload the large sheets of glass from the trucks delivering the glass and place the glass in the proper bins. Subsequently the same system would enable them to send the computer arm to the sheet of glass and bring that sheet to the cutting table. Huge suction cups were used to grab the glass.

With no one buying, Mitsubishi called upon Conrad to see if he was interested in buying back his business/. Conrad made what I thought was a ridiculous offer of $750,000. They accepted the offer and Conrad was back in business. He went back to work and started getting back the customers they had lost. This time he built it up to the point where the business was showing a profit and I was back in the accounting saddle again with Conrad.

Conrad was not too happy working full time again and put the business up for sale again. He found a nationwide company, who is listed in the New York Stock Exchange, who wanted to come into the local area. This time Conrad only sold the business and retained the real estate. He sold the business for millions again and signed a long-term triple net lease with the tenant.

Conrad collected the rent for several years and then a potential customer came along to buy the real estate. A sale was arranged and Conrad was out completely again.

As I mentioned previously, Conrad had great mechanical abilities. He always owned at least one airplane and he had built a hanger and runway on the farm He now came up with the idea to build his own airplane. He bought a kit and went to work building his airplane. He did more than just follow the instructions that came with the kit. He embellished and elaborated the basic design and added all sorts of electronics. When the plane was finished, he flew it out to Oshkosh to the annual air show. He won first prize for the best home built plane, which was quite a feat. I flew with Conrad on almost every trip I made to Warrenton. He would let me take control of the plane once we up in the sky and he taught me how to fly circles without deviating the height by more than a hundred feet.

Conrad made some additional improvements in the plane and won first prize again the following year. Then came the time when Conrad wanted to sell the plane. He found out that it was not saleable. I suspected he knew that all along. Since it was an experimental plane, no buyer could get insurance. I discussed with Conrad that he negotiate with an aircraft museum to see if they wanted his plane. He found a museum in Florida who would take the plane and give him a charitable contribution receipt for just about what he had spent on the plane. I deducted the contribution on his tax return that year and sent in the documentation he had received from the museum. The Internal Revenue Service never questioned the contribution.

Kiyoshi and his family went back to Japan for a while. He had two daughters and the younger one came to New York to visit with us one summer for a few weeks. Kiyoshi was sent to Hong Kong by Mitsubishi and became the manager of a coated paper business doing millions of dollars of business. My wife and I booked a trip to China and it included a few days in Hong Kong at the end of the trip. I wrote to Kiyoshi and told him when we would be in Hong Kong and then had to leave on the trip before I received a reply from him.

We had a great time in China especially seeing the terra cotta soldiers in Xian and the Great Wall. Our guide was a gorgeous young Chinese lady who had us up every morning a 6 AM to do Ti Chi. We were 15 on the trip and only my wife remained in bed each morning. We always had an audience who giggled watching us perform.

When we got to Hong Kong I almost did not bother to try to contact Kiyoshi because since I had not heard from him, I thought perhaps he did not want to bother with me any longer. Anyway, I did look up the Mitsubishi office on Star Island and spoke to Kiyoshi. He was delighted to hear from me. He told me that as soon as he got my letter, he immediately called my office in New York and found out from my secretary that we had already left on our trip. He asked if Frances and I would have dinner with him that night. He would send a car for us. Frances and I waited in front of our hotel with the rest of our group as they were all going to a restaurant. The car he had sent for us showed up while the rest of the group was still there. They were shocked when they saw the chauffeured Daimler arrive. We were taken to his apartment on the other side of Hong Kong Island in an apartment building called The Manhattan. Again it was off with the shoes and a fabulous dinner prepared by his wife. She cooked most of the meat at the table.

Kiyoshi invited me to join him at his office for lunch the next day. I told Frances to come with me but my wife is smarter than I am and told me to go without her. She was right. At his office Kiyoshi introduced me to many of his coworkers. We went to lunch in a private club and there were only men there, as Frances suspected. The lunch was delicious and served beautifully. That night Kiyoshi and his wife took us to a Chinese restaurant. It was fabulous seeing him and his family again. We have remained in touch by e-mail and Christmas cards through the years. He is now retired and living in Yokohama.

As we were leaving him in Hong Kong, he offered to have his brother meet us at the Tokyo airport and take us into Tokyo to show us the city. We had to stop in Narita airport on the way home. I asked Kiyoshi if his brother spoke any English. He said "not a word." I thanked him for his kind offer but turned him down.

He then suggested that when we are in Narita Airport that we take a cab to the town of Narita and go to see a lovely Japanese shrine. We followed his advice and went with six other people on the tour to Narita and saw the shrine. It then came time to have dinner and I motioned to a Japanese man standing in the street that we were hungry by waving my hand in front of my mouth. He understood the gesture and waved us to a small restaurant. We all went into the restaurant and had a great meal.

The owner, a woman and the waitresses were dressed in traditional Japanese costumes. The only other customers were two FedEx pilots. I got into a discussion with the woman who owned the restaurant and we had a lovely long conversation and became friendly. She told me that the next time we come to Japan we must stay with her. When it became time to head back to the motel, I asked her to call for two cabs for us. She then spoke to her cook and he came around with a large station wagon and drove us all back to our motel. The owner admonished me not to give the cook a tip. I eventually told Kiyoshi about our lovely evening based on his suggestion.

A client of mine, who is an author, told me that he would like to write a book from a Japanese serviceman's point of view. I told him about Kiyoshi and he asked me if I would contact him. I did and his reply was that he had relatives who died in the atomic bomb blast and could not help.

Another of our literary agents is a lovely Japanese lady; Hiroko K. She too has been a client of mine for many years. She was in partnership with another lady for a while and then her partner moved away from New York. Hiroko has specialized in authors who write cookbooks. She had struggled to earn substantial funds for herself and fortunately for her, her husband is a successful architect. A few years ago Hiroko acquired a young lady as a client who has gone on to make a huge success for herself. The author of whom I speak is none other than the now famous Rachel Ray. Hiroko did wonderfully for Rachel and herself for a few years. As is common in almost all cases where an individual represents a person who becomes a successful star, they lose the star to a much larger organization. That is exactly what happened to Hiroko. I know that Hiroko is not really upset about losing Rachel Ray, because I am sure she knew that it was inevitable. I will say that Rachel has acknowledged on television her successful relationship with Hiroko and has spoken of Hiroko in glowing terms.

A Vacation Results In Acquiring A Client.

Usually when I go on vacation with my wife, and we have taken many vacations to foreign lands, I always tell the strangers we meet who inquire what I do for a living, that I sell ladies shoes. One character actually asked me what lines I carry. Obviously, the reason I do not tell people that I am a CPA is because the strangers usually have a friend with a tax question or a tax problem. I am on vacation and the last thing I want to do is discuss taxation.

We were on our first trip to Israel and we met a lovely couple from Fort Lee, New Jersey. We became very friendly with them and I eventually told Leon that I am a CPA.

I was working at Allegheny Freight Lines in Winchester, Virginia and I received a call from Leon. He knew that I was out of town and insisted on knowing when I would be coming back to New York. I asked what was so urgent and he said, "They just locked up my accountant and his son." Leon was in the business of manufacturing steel partitions, usually used in bathrooms and offices. He did have his own factory at one point but now he had others manufacture the partitions and he just installed them. His wife owned a couple of variety stores in New Jersey and I became the accountant for both of them. We subsequently went on vacation with them to Portugal and Leon died a few years ago and his wife Florence died quite recently.

After she passed away her daughter and son in law were in touch with me to discuss her tax affairs. Tax season recently came to an end and I had not heard from Florence's family. I spoke to the son in law and he told me that the girls have used their accountant. I said to him that it would have been the decent thing to call me and advise me of their decision. He apologized on their behalf. Unfortunately, too many people are just thoughtless.

In the same shopping center, where Leon's wife Florence had one of her stores, was a delicatessen. I became friendly with Kenny the owner. When he opened a Bagel Nosh in Fort Lee, I became his accountant. At that point the Bagel Nosh was a small chain of stores and they were franchised. Oddly enough, the owner of the franchises was an Italian. All the stores were similarly decorated. Unfortunately, bagels were not as popular then as they are right now and Kenny failed. The failure was partially caused by the exorbitant monthly franchise fee and the supplies that were purchased from the franchiser.

Kenny then opened a deli elsewhere in New Jersey. His wife was the bookkeeper and sadly she died of cancer a few years ago. Kenny has since moved to Florida. I prepared his tax returns until last year when I lost contact with him.

Excellent Kosher Meals Comes With The Territory

I am sure that very few people have heard of Areles Restaurant. They were a kosher restaurant and nightclub on the lower east side of Manhattan for many years. I had as clients a wedding photographer and a photo-processing laboratory for wedding photographers in Flushing. Harold had referred them both to me. Harold had worked with me while I was with Max Steiner. Harold, who was as knowledgeable with the trucking industry as I was, became the controller for a large moving and storage company in New York. He was a boyhood friend with the owners of the wedding photographer and the laboratory and recommended them to me as clients.

The wedding photographer was the "official" photographer for Areles, who had now moved from the lower east side to Flushing on the Long Island Expressway.

Working for Areles was a real challenge. The owners were a Jewish man, whose father started the business many years ago and whose name was Arele. The other owner, Joseph was an Italian gentleman who spoke Yiddish and knew all about kosher catering and cooking. Strangely enough, the chef was Japanese whose name was Johnny Yashikowa. The chef and the misgiach (the rabbi on the premises, in charge of seeing that the food he is serving was strictly kosher) were constantly arguing. Not about the food, but about the soap being used to wash the dishes to determine if the soap was kosher.

On the record, Areles never made any money and struggled to pay the bills. Nat G. the Jewish owner was a gambler and a ladies' man and that was the cause of all his problems. Eventually they had to close their doors and today the place is occupied by a funeral home.

While I had them as a client, my wife and I enjoyed eating there. We would go to the Metropolitan Opera on a Saturday evening and on the way home, would drop in to Areles for a late dinner and a show. Their food was excellent and the sweetbreads were unreal. We celebrated our twentieth anniversary there and had a lovely party with relatives and friends.

The bookkeeper, Mildred at Areles was excellent but working there gave her nothing but aggravation. Her husband, Percy manufactured ladies undies and after a while I became his accountant as well. That went on for a few years and Percy failed and his wife died.

I continued to prepare Percy's tax returns. Percy moved to Florida and continued to send me his tax information. He met a woman there and married her. Percy called me and apologized profusely and told me that he would have to use her accountant from now on. I told Percy that the fact that he took the time to call me and felt badly that he was making a change, more than compensated for the fact that I was losing him as a client. He was a gentleman and I loved him for the fact that he bothered to call and not just disappeared.

My wife and I had friends who were both close friends and clients. It was just a tax return. Julie had worked for all the major TV stations in their taping departments. Over the years he "stole" pieces of film that contained celebrities. When he retired he thought he would make a fortune out of selling his "library". No one was interested because they could not get proper releases. He died of cancer and his wife spent several evenings at our home going over her finances and planning for her future, for which I never billed her. That year during the tax season as usual I got so busy that I did not realize that I had not heard from Bunny. I would not call her and just waited to hear from her. She never called to say that she was changing accountants. When my wife asked her, after tax season was over, why she had not called me to tell me what she was doing, Bunny told my wife that she had called me to advise me of her decision. She lied because she was embarrassed. I have a terrible memory when it comes to something like that and I have not spoken to Bunny since. Why people cannot do the decent thing is something I do not understand. I guess that she was just ashamed of what she was doing and could not bring herself to call me. It was only a one hundred-dollar tax return, so it was not something that I could not live without.

Another Huge Disappointment

One of my biggest disappointments in my accounting career was when a client that I had nurtured, advised and lived with for many years dumped me. The client was DeVore Aviation. Gilbert DeVore and his partner Arnold Robinson were two brilliant aeronautical engineers. Their specialty at the beginning of their careers was helicopters. They both lived in Bayside Queens, which is where I live and therefore they were neighbors. I have always intended to record on each client's records, the person who recommended them to me. Unfortunately, I have never gotten around to doing it. So, I really do not remember how DeVore Aviation became a client. They might have been recommended by their attorney.

They got started on Bell Blvd, a busy shopping street in Bayside. Their first office was probably 500 square feet on the second floor of the building, with a store underneath.

Their work came to them through their reputation in the aviation field. I do not remember the entire sequence of events but their biggest break came when Hugh Hefner of Playboy Clubs and magazines purchased an airplane. He had it painted black and had a bunny, his signature piece, painted on the upright tail of the plane. Someone suggested to him to contact DeVore Aviation to get the job done of lighting up the bunny. When it comes to adding to and changing anything on an airplane, it becomes a major project requiring engineering and many approvals from governmental agencies. Gilbert and Arnold worked on this project and figured out how to install lights in the wingtips of the plane and have them light up the bunny. After several months they got the required approval. The biggest problem, which they solved, was the heat generated by the lights and the nearby fuel tanks. They received the Certificate of Approval for the lights. They got paid; I think $50,000 for the work they did. Even though Mr. Hefner paid for the project and technically owned the Certificate of Approval, nevertheless the certificate was issued to DeVore Aviation.

Immediately Gilbert solicited all the airlines, which owned the same plane that belonged to Playboy, for orders for lights. I am not certain but the plane may have been a DC3 or a DC4. Playboy wanted the lights strictly for advertising purposes and it might have some appeal for the airlines for the same purpose. However, the lighted tails of the planes were really a safety factor since the control tower could more easily spot the planes on the runways

TWA airlines ordered 250 light sets. Gilbert and Arnold were ecstatic. This was a huge profitable order and they were off and running. They had a huge party for the staff and several others. They moved their office to Roslyn, NY to a nice spacious office. As I said earlier, they were two smart cookies and they immediately began work on getting lights certificated for all the planes that were being flown by the airlines. It was a project that was very labor intensive. To obtain these certificates costs thousands of dollars in payroll, but they became so successful that the plane manufacturers at first placed orders with them to add the lights to their planes. Of course the plane manufacturers began to create their own light systems. Gilbert decided to create lights for all planes flying that were also owned by corporations and individuals. There the cost of creating these lights far exceeded the sales created.

Another of their projects was for I think it was Cornell. They created a computer system that was placed in an airplane. The computer could be adjusted to create the feeling that while flying that particular plane the pilot felt as if he was flying any plane that was in service at that time. Obviously it was a great device for training airline pilots. It enabled pilots to learn how to fly the newest and largest planes without actually tying them up for training.

They purchased plans for aircraft floats from a recently widowed lady. Most people call the planes that they see land on water "seaplanes" Actually seaplanes are those whose body's land on the water. The planes that we see land on floats and are called floatplanes. The floats are made up of watertight sections. They are attached to planes that have had their landing wheels and connections removed and replaced with the floats. A floatplane obviously requires a plane with a very strong engine in order to lift off from the water. Gilbert and Arnold got into the business with both hands and actually started manufacturing the floats.

Once again, to get each set of floats certificated required thousands of dollars of labor. Floats planes are common in only certain areas of the country. Namely, Alaska, Louisiana, New York and those states bordering on the Great Lakes. Gilbert was never one to do things half-heartedly and began to get certificates for any plane that could fly with floats. The next step was to create amphibious floats, which they did. Amphibious floats can land at a normal airport or on water. The wheels are extended or withdrawn with hydraulic pumps. Many times the floats cost more that the airplanes to which they are attached.

Gilbert and Arnold kept expanding the lines they developed and opened places in New England and California to manufacture their products. Some of the additional products they developed were a system that attaches to helicopters to cut the overhead wires that the helicopter encounters when flying low, a box that sits at the end of a runway of a small airport that emits a variety of light signals that notifies the pilot who is landing that he is too high, too low, too far to the left or right and a parking system for aircraft, plus other projects.

Gilbert and Arnold went public with their corporation and raised $300,000. They gave me a number of shares for my efforts in helping their company grow and succeed. I could not do the accounting for the public issue and turned it over to my friend and neighbor. Paul was a partner in a larger accounting firm and he also taught at City College.

I went with them to Puerto Rico when they were engaged by Carib Air to review their systems and I went along to look at their accounting systems. I went out to Coffeyville Kansas with them where they were reviewing the engineering of a company and I looked at the accounting. To say that we were close would be an understatement.

Eventually they started to investigate the possibility of consolidating their operation into one location. Gilbert went out west and interviewed the Chambers of Commerce of several cities and settled on Albuquerque, New Mexico. They moved there and set up shop to manufacture all of their products.

Then Gilbert and Arnold purchased the plans from an English firm to manufacture a small all plastic simple plane basically to be used to teach people to fly. In theory it sounded great but it turned out to be a major fiasco. Two million dollars were expended and when all was said and done, the planes could not be sold because any potential purchaser could not get insurance.

When they were still located in New York, Gilbert allowed me and my family to spend a week or so at a home he owned in Falmouth on Cape Cod. At the end of our stay we went down to the pier to meet Gilbert and his son who had been out sailing. As Gilbert jumped off the sailboat he handed a line to my nine-year daughter Susan. He told her to hold on to the rope securely. After Gilbert and his son were off the boat, it started to drift out to sea. He turned to my daughter and screamed at the top of his lungs, "I told you to hold onto the rope." She said, "I am holding onto the rope, you forgot to tie it onto the boat." That was Gilbert at his best.

Gilbert's wife died at an early age and he remarried twice more. One of the women he was dating went on vacation with him to Spain, I believe before they married. As they were coming through customs, they were asked if they had anything to declare. He and his lady said they did not. The custom officer asked Gilbert to open the leather envelope he was holding under his arm. In the envelope were all the receipts for the thousands of dollars for things they had purchased in Spain. The custom officer asked if perhaps they wanted to change their declaration. With that, the lady opened up her mouth and started yelling that she was a U. S. citizen and should not be persecuted, etc. The custom officer called over a woman officer and Gilbert and the lady were escorted to private rooms, stripped and searched. All the things they purchased were confiscated and they had to engage an attorney and appear in court. I asked Gilbert what this all cost and he said, "Shut up."

Once Gilbert came to my office for a meeting. He had with him his European leather purse, which he left behind on my desk. A few hours later he called all excited and wanted to know if he had left his purse in my office. I asked him, "Did you notice you were missing the purse when you went looking for your lipstick?" Again he said, "Shut up." But Gilbert and I were great friends and I stayed at his him home when I went to Albuquerque.

Their salesman, Dan Carp did not move to Albuquerque with them and stayed in New York. We rented Dan a desk in our office from which he operated.

After going to Albuquerque for about two years, I was told by Gilbert, while he was driving me back to the airport, that my services were no longer required. Gilbert was always impressed with wealth and wealthy people. He longed to advance himself in society. He had joined a golf club and I can only assume he became impressed with an accountant he had met at the golf club. I did not even try to talk him out of his decision and I knew Gilbert well enough to know that all the years we had worked and struggled together meant nothing to him when all was said and done. It hurt but c'est la vie.

I had some of my friends buy stock in DeVore Aviation at $5 a share when they went public. After I was no longer their accountant, my friends and I received notice of a reverse split of the stock of 1 share to be issued for every 10 currently owned. Then subsequently a notice arrived that anyone with less than 100 shares had to turn in their shares for $1 each. In the end, apparently DeVore turned crooked and probably had a customer for his business and wanted to get rid of all the little stockholders. I just felt badly that I had induced my friends to invest.

More Interesting Clients

Kenny R., the world famous photographer, had a lady friend, Deborah P. She worked for MONEY magazine. I met her and become her accountant. She interviewed me for a tax article she was writing for the magazine. The interview went on for about a half hour. When the magazine appeared, I was named and quoted with a nine or ten word quote.

She wanted to get married but Kenny had been married previously and was not interested in marrying again. They parted company.

Deborah then became friendly with John H. John ran a school for would be creators and builders of fine furniture. People from all walks of life attended his school. By sheer coincidence, one of his talented pupils was my client Susan M. the book packager. She had built a beautiful dining room table.

John was so successful in teaching his students that a few of them opened up their own schools in direct competition with him. I had become his accountant as well. His next endeavor was to sell exotic rare woods from all over the world. That worked for a while but there was not enough of a demand for his product.

Somewhere along the line John and Deborah married. They had a son and as happens in too many marriages these days, they divorced after a few years.

John never let any grass grow under his feet and he opened up a business of selling imported tools. The tools mostly came from Japan. He obtained an 800 number from Verizon. As fate would have it, the same number was assigned to a television station in California. They were running a contest and John was receiving many calls every day from people wanting to enter the contest. Each erroneous call was costing John one dollar. John was certain that he had obtained the 800 number before the television station. He called Verizon and they did nothing. He called the television station and they said they would not change the number. John was not born yesterday. From that point on, every person calling who thought they were calling the television station, were told by John that they had won the prize and they should immediately go to the television station to claim their prize. John must have referred several hundred people to go and pick up their prize.

Needless to say, the television station called him and begged him to stop what he was doing. John told them that all they had to do was change their 800 number. Of course they did as soon as possible

John never sat still. He created a photo studio with the unique abilities to satisfy professional photographer's needs. He rented the space to photographers and that succeeded for a while.

That enterprise came to an end as well. John supports himself currently by consulting with several equipment manufacturers. He is a very knowledgeable engineer.

He also creates plans of apartments that are for rent or for sale. His clients are the large real estate agents in Manhattan. One of the largest real estate agency requested that John increase the size of the apartment to an amount larger than the actual square footage. He said he could not do it because he could subject himself to a possible lawsuit and the agency would just say that the relied on him. Unfortunately they stopped using his services.

His most current enterprise is building a soft ice cream machine that delivers a variety of flavors from the one machine and will automatically clean itself the end of the day. He has received patents and has been having a difficult time in creating a prototype but he is not deterred.

Betty B. was an executive with HBO. She had a huge corner office in New York on Sixth Avenue and 43rd Street. Betty was the person in charge of producing the live shows. I know she did the Billy Joel show in Moscow a number of years ago. She was making a handsome salary when she decided to quit. They begged her to stay.

She tried her hand at a couple of businesses but none of them succeeded. She has since moved out west and she still sends me her information for her tax returns.

Karl M. and Shareen B. are married and are both authors, Karl is the brother of Susan M. and was written about on the front page of the METRO section of the New York Times. They travel and do their research extensively and are both successful.

Ralph Di. is a city planner. He was employed by New York City and then branched out into his business. He has projects with several of the small cities in New York State.

I have as a tax client, a lovely lady, who unfortunately lost her husband in the September 11th disaster. She was recommended by my financial advisor and we have jointly assisted her in setting up trusts for her children with the funds she received.

Gloria G. is a widow of many years. She was a client of an attorney for whom I used to do some work. When he passed away, his law firm received court approval for me to become the successor trustee of the two trusts that were created by her husband's will.

The Clients I Have Never Met.

I have never met many of the people for whom I prepare tax returns. They have been recommended to me and I speak with them on the phone. They then mail their information to me. I prepare their returns, mail them back to them with an invoice and hopefully get paid for my endeavors. Some of these clients have been with me for many years. I would not know them if I passed them in the street.

One client, whom I had met once, has remained with me and went on to become a business client when he left his job and went into business for himself. I had not seen him in many years. Once while Fred and I were flying home from Washington, We were at the National Airport, after having worked in Virginia, I spotted this gentleman waiting for his plane. I turned to Fred and told him to watch me. I walked up to my client and said, "How are you Dr. M.?" He said, "Who are you?" I told him that I was his accountant and he nearly flipped.

Dr. M is another of my genius clients. He is not a medical doctor but has his doctorate in the medical field. He taught anatomy at Mount Sinai hospital. While working at the hospital he thought up the idea of creating a medical Lexus. He, and I believe another coworker, developed a computer system wherein a doctor, attending to a patient, would enter into the computer program the symptoms that the patient was suffering. The computer would then advise the doctor of the possible malady and what tests should be undertaken. He went into business and succeeded in selling the programs to doctors and soon thereafter sold the company for a substantial gain.

Dr. M. cannot sit idle and soon thereafter, came up with this idea. He hired several highly intelligent men and women, with medical backgrounds, who had their doctorates. They would read the highly technical medical articles appearing in the New England Journal of Medicine and other technical publications. They would then rewrite the articles in laymen's terms and sell their service. I asked Dr. M who would purchase his products and he said, "Doctors of course." This too became a successful enterprise for my client. Once again he was successful in selling the business for a substantial gain.

Unfortunately, his wife died of leukemia. He did everything in his power to aid her and they even went to California for a bone marrow transplant. He eventually remarried another lovely intelligent woman and as I have said previously, not only are they clients but they are also good friends. He is now working for a large company that is utilizing his skills.

A Client's Wife Uncovers My Artistic Ability

I have another client, who is really a doctor. Our mutual attorney recommended him to me. I called him and arranged to meet him at his office. He is a psychiatrist and asked me to be at his office at ten minutes to two. I was there on time and we spoke for perhaps twelve or thirteen minutes and he agreed to engage my services. When I went out into the waiting room, the next patient was sitting there chewing his fingernails as I had used up two or three minutes of his session.

Dr. F continues to be a valuable client. He had a bookkeeper, who I recommended, write up his records. She moved from New York and we took over her function. He mails his information to our office and we record his income and expenditures in our computer program. We do this procedure for a few clients. I prefer going to the client's place of business to perform my work. I know that there are many, what I call, pick and up and delivery accounting firms. They send a staff member to the client to pick up the bank statements and other relevant material. They then record the information in the accountant's office and return the material back to the client on their next visit. There is no genuine personal contact, discussion and advice. Now, that kind of accounting is boring.

Dr F.'s wife is a recognized artist. She has her own studio and displays her work in a gallery. She also taught a class on tombstone rubbings. I attended the class and she took us to Trinity Church to learn how to rub the tombstones to obtain a picture of the inscription on the tombstone. The next session was in front of the Museum of Natural History where we rubbed sewer covers. I became hooked on rubbing. I have been to England and made rubbings of some of the brass plates covering the tombstones in Westminster Abbey and other churches. I did this many years ago and they no longer allow people to rub in Westminster Abbey. There is a shop close by, where they have replicas of the brass plates and people pay a fee to make their rubbings. I did a rubbing in a small country church and paid a small fee for the privilege. While I was rubbing, the priest would pop in every few minutes to check up on me to make certain that I was alone. Apparently, other people had paid one fee but had their friend join them to rub.

Gary S and his wife Victoria was another interesting client. Victoria was from England and Gary would have loved to acquire an English accent. He was a talented artist and if some of you are old enough to remember drawings in the subway that were placed there by the New York Times. The theme was "it goes to your head." Gary created the works of art. I have one in my office.

In addition to his artistic endeavors, Gary and Victoria ran a business of selling Italian furniture in the Designers and Decorators building in New York. It was a struggle for them and they never really succeeded financially. Gary's other claim to fame was the fact that he created and sold a diary to architects. He did this annually and really turned out lovely diaries and sold them to a repeat list of customers. Gary had been a Marine and decided to create a diary that he would sell to ex-marines and those still in service in the Marine Corp. It never became as successful as the architect's diary but Gary lived in hope and I know he suffered in despair. Gary and Victoria had their own ideas about filing tax returns and paying taxes and we came to a parting of the way.

The Italian Connection.

One of the last trucking companies that I had as a client was a relatively small trucking company with their office in the lower West Side of Manhattan. The owner was John B. He was well trained in running a trucking company and was financially successful. He hired a young Indian man to do the clerical and bookkeeping work. On the first time that I met him, he said to me, "you will do my tax returns" in his lilting Indian voice. I replied, "No, I will not do your tax returns." He wanted to know why I would not prepare his tax returns and I told him that I do not do tax returns for the bookkeepers. His wife worked around the corner and brought him his Indian lunch every day. Apparently, according to their religion, there were days when he would eat and she would fast. Occasionally I would taste what she had brought for him. I did not care for the food.

John's landlord sold the garage that John used as an office and terminal. Instead of John looking for another place of business, he decided to close his doors and retire. John lived in Brooklyn and I had to go to his home several times to wind up the bookkeeping affairs of his company. John was Italian and when it came lunchtime, he and I would go to the store "club" for lunch. It was I suppose a typical Italian club, of which there are many in New York. There were card games in progress. A bar to serve drinks and facilities to cook and prepare food. The food was delicious and I enjoyed spending a couple of hours with John and his friends.

The French Connection.

I had a real Italian Don as a client. He was a fabulous individual and the nicest man you would ever know. I loved him. I call him a Don because his entire family, of which there were many members, always came to him for advice and directions. I knew him from the time I worked for Wasserman and Taten. He was employed by one of their clients and then branched out on his own. He imported tie silk piece goods from Italy and his two brothers Mario and Cosmo were in the business with him. George Sr. had at least two sisters and a family of his own. He had two sons George Jr. and Joseph and a daughter. My wife and I attended all the family functions and weddings.

I became George's accountant. When it came time to gather the information to file the tax returns for the family, Fred and I would go to George's house in Manhasset. We would sit at the table on the porch and each member of the family would sit with us to give us their information. This was at a time when there were no form 1099s from the banks and brokers. George, Sr. would stand at the table and every time an item came up as to whether or not it should be reported in the tax return, George Sr. said, "put it down". When we had finished our work with the entire family, Mrs. George served a fantastic Italian lunch with all the traditional dishes. Fred and I always looked forward to our annual visit.

George was a very charitable man and donated to the Christian Brothers. Each year he would pay for one or two tables at their annual dinner. Frances and I were always invited. There was always a clergyman at each table. We were always fortunate to sit at the table with the President of Manhattan College.

Many of the people in the tie manufacturing and tie piece goods trade were Jewish. George spoke Yiddish and was honored by the United Jewish Appeal for his involvement in Jewish life. George also made contributions to other Jewish organizations and when he died, several orthodox rabbis came to pay their respect at the funeral home.

In addition to buying tie silk material and reselling it to tie manufacturers, George also represented silk mills in France and Italy on a commission basis. One of the firms that he represented was located in Lyon, France. The owner Jacque D. had decided to open up an office in New York and hire his own salesman. I had met Jacques on several occasions, namely at Joseph's wedding and other family functions. George, being the good friend that he was, suggested to Jacques that if he was going into business, he would need an accountant and suggested that he contact me, Jacques did call me and I began working for him. Jacques and his family own a large textile mill and sell their products worldwide. Money is no object for Jacques. He formed two corporations. One to sell their regular products to tie manufacturers and the other to create logos for large corporations to be made into neckties. He was not interested in renting an office and immediately purchased two apartments. One on 38th Street between Park and Madison Avenues and the other on 57th Street west of Broadway. Jacques comes to New York several times a year to see his customers. We usually meet for lunch or dinner when he is here.

Jacques has customers in New Orleans, California and points in between. He and his wife have traveled the U. S. extensively and have probably seen more of our country than most Americans.

After the war ended I went on furlough to Switzerland with my friend Jack Kurtz. We spent three weeks there. We were allowed to bring in $35. Jack and I brought a duffel bag full of cigarettes and spare clothing and sold them all. I always vowed that someday I would go back to Switzerland and so I did with my wife. We had a grand time revisiting the places I had been in 1945. We then drove to Lyon to see Jacques. On the way to Lyon, we stopped at the town of Vonnais. A stockbroker had suggested we eat in a restaurant called George Blanc in the town of Vonnais. He said it was expensive and said he would pick up the tab if we were not thrilled with the place. George Blanc is a five star restaurant. We had difficulty finding the town because I thought the broker had said Bonnais. We had stopped in at a gas station to ask for directions and were told that there is no Bonnais, but when I told him we were seeking George Blanc, he gave us directions.

We stopped at the restaurant and asked if we could have dinner that evening. We were asked if we had a reservation. We did not and were told one has to book weeks in advance, however, good fortune smiled on us, and there was a cancellation which we could have. There was no room in the hotel in town and we were sent about 10 miles away to a lovely guesthouse, which we enjoyed tremendously. We asked for a reservation at 7 PM and the reservation clerk said, "Sir you have the table for the entire evening." The dinner was, as predicted, very expensive but worth every penny. At 10 PM George Blanc came into the dining room and sat and chatted with all the patrons. It was like he owned the entire town. There was a landing strip and helicopter pad on the edge of town to accommodate his customers.

We proceeded on to Lyon. Jacques gave us a tour of the mill. If you have been to a textile mill you would really enjoy seeing his mill. It was the most modern of all mills with many Jacquard looms. Jacquard looms weave the pattern into the goods. The directions to the loom are large cards with holes punched in the cards to direct which strands of the warp are to be lifted or depressed and when the shuttle should cross across the loom with the woof thread. It is much like a player piano.

Jacques took the day off from work just to be with us. He took us to lunch and then a ride in the country to his home. He was a gracious host. He took us to dinner at a fabulous restaurant in Lyon. We told him about our visit to George Blanc. He had heard about the place but had never been there and promised to go. He and his lovely wife have been to our home in the Hamptons.

George was a generous man and when one of his friends Ernest R. needed some funds, George loaned him $20,000. Ernest was also in the tie trade. George took out a life insurance policy on Ernest's life to guarantee repayment in the event of his death. Ernest was a client of mine as well. He and two others Sidney D. and John M. were tie silk converters. Ernest made his payments diligently but it was almost like his death was predicted before paying off the entire loan. Ernest died still owing George about half the loan. George collected on the life insurance and being the gentleman that he was, instead of keeping the entire $20,000, he gave Ernest's widow all the money that Ernest had paid to George in liquidating the loan.

After George Senior passed away, his sons George Jr and Joseph kept the business going for a few years. People are wearing less and less ties and all the tie manufacturers and textile converters suffered and many went out of business.

Joseph came to the office annually to bring us the information for his tax return. It was always on a Saturday and that date also turned into an Italian feast. Joseph would show up with shopping bags full of meats, cheeses and breads. Joseph was obese and sadly died at an early age. We all miss him. I continued to work for his widow for two years and then she met a man and went to his accountant. Perhaps, at this point she had married him. George Jr. still comes to us. Mario and Cosmo passed away a few years ago. Marie, George Sr's sister works for Jacques D. and answers his phone and processes the orders here in New York.

My Oldest Client.

Edward W. had worked for the furrier I had mentioned previously. He left his job and joined forces with Herbert T., a friend of his who was a designer. They opened up a business selling ladies fur-trimmed suits. The designs were good and Edward was a good salesman. Business prospered.

Edward came to me one day and told me that he was getting married and I was not to tell his partner what would be in the joint tax returns that he and his wife will be filing. I told Edward that I had been preparing his partner's returns for several years and never divulged to him what was in the joint return that I filed for Herbert and his wife. Edward said, "OK, but you will see what I mean later." Edward was in his early 40s when he got married.

When tax season came along, Edward and his wife Ruth came to my office. Edward was carrying three ledgers, each about three inches thick. He set them down on my desk and Ruth began reading to me the name of corporate stock she owned and the dividend received the previous year. Again, this was so many years ago that 1099 form did not exist as yet. She read page after page and I copied down the information as she read it to me.

When she finally had gone through all three ledgers, we then discussed the other items to be used in the preparation of their joint returns. I asked her for a copy of her previous year's tax returns, which she handed to me. Obviously, I was curious to know who prepared the returns and how much he had charged. There was no indication on the returns as to who had prepared them, nor was there a deduction for tax preparation.

I asked Ruth who prepared the tax returns? She said that she had gone to the Internal Revenue Office with her records and they helped her prepare the return. This was at a time when the IRS would do that. Today they only help people with low incomes. I asked her if she might not have been better off seeing an accountant, who would make some decisions in her favor rather than an Internal Revenue Agent who took no interest in her affairs. She told me that she had stood on three separate lines and had three different agents' help her and she then filed the return with the best tax advantage for her. She said she had spent an entire day at the Internal Revenue. Smart lady, right?

Ruth's father had been a Certified Public Accountant and had a very low certificate number. He had divorced her mother and had set up a trust for Ruth. Edward is a number of years older than Ruth, but I still cater to them. Edward sends me his information annually from Florida and he is well into his 90s at this time. His information arrived this year, neatly arranged and complete with the information needed to prepare their joint returns. Annually I have to call his son Peter, his stockbroker, to obtain the cost of the securities sold.

The Union Destroys A Client.

Harold F, his wife the bookkeeper and his son James became clients. They came as a result of Harold's wife being friendly with one of the bookkeepers at a client of mine. They operated their business in the Park Slope section of Brooklyn. They dealt in glass. They purchased the large sheet of glass in various thicknesses ranging from one sixteenth of an inch to one inch. They made tabletops, shelves and a host of other products. They had been in business for many years and everyone in the trade knew of them. They only had about a dozen employees and they were a unionized shop. Most of their competitors were non union shops. But, Harold knew how to deal with the union requests and succeeded in spite of the additional burden placed on the finances of the company because of the union pension and welfare costs. Harold was a very sweet man and well liked by all who knew him. He passed away untimely and his son and daughter in law took over the business.

The union contract came up for renewal and James fought the union. The union did despicable things like following his trucks to the jobs and puncturing the truck tires. They picketed outside his shop. All James wanted them to do was to organize his competitors, but they would not listen to him. He told them that if they put him out of business, his employees would all lose their jobs and that threat did not shake them. James hired lawyers, who charged big fees and accomplished absolutely nothing. Instead of settling with the union, as his father would have done, James was obstinate and it became inevitable that he would have to close his doors, which he did.

James and his wife were opera lovers and attended at least one opera a week. Whenever we went to the opera we would always see him and his wife in the Belmont Room. James's wife died at an early age and he lived with his daughter. I continued to do his tax work until his daughter, who had moved upstate New York with James wrote me and told me that James now had Alzheimer's disease and did not know anyone any longer.

My Investment Councilor Is A Great Source Of Business.

My investment advisor, Ruth S., who hates when I call her my stockbroker, has over the years recommended several wealthy ladies as clients. Again, some of these women I have never met. But, apparently her suggestion that I become these ladies accountant, is good enough for them. Over and above these ladies, Ruth recommended a law firm, for whom she handles their pension account. These were four Irish men whose office is in the Bronx. It was a father, a son and the son's two friends. I think the young men all knew each other having been assistant district attorneys in the Bronx. They had an Irish accountant who was always filing their tax returns late and they were continually receiving late notices with penalties and interest charges. I promised that I would put an end to that for them and give them my expert service. I began working for them and saw to it that all their filings were done timely. The father Patrick L. W. would take me to lunch at Louie's, where he had his lunchtime cocktail and we both usually had a fish dish for an entrée.

I have always told my wife how much I enjoyed going to work in the Bronx with these men. We always joked and kidded around and the time spent there was most pleasurable. Patrick L. passed away and his son Patrick J. continued on with his partners. After some time Patrick J. parted company with Charles S. and Marc S. They all remained in the same office and are still friends, but Patrick J. felt he could do much better financial if he went off by himself and it has turned out to be true.

I remain the accountant for all three men. My daughter, Amy, the CPA comes to their office to do their bookkeeping for Charles S and Marc S. Patrick J. does his own entries in his computer. I have turned over to Amy several clients so that they have expert bookkeeping services. I do not bill these clients for Amy's services and they pay her directly. One client was looking for a part time bookkeeper and I suggested my daughter. She was shocked. That would be nepotism she said, so I told her to forget it. After going through a couple of incompetent bookkeepers, she called me and told me to have Amy call her. Amy went on to do her work and she loved Amy, as do all of her clients.

Charles S. unfortunately has a daughter who is terribly physically handicapped from birth. She requires round the clock nursing aid. After many years, the family was finally awarded a substantial settlement for the damaged inflicted on their daughter at the hospital. I have to prepare annually for the court an accounting detailing the income received and the expenditures on her behalf.

Over the last two or three years, I have been working very closely with Patrick J. He has clients dying and leaving substantial estates from time to time. He does the legal work and allows me to do the accounting for the estates and preparing and filing the federal and New York State Inheritance Tax Returns. It is lucrative work for him and me and we work very well as a team. An attorney friend of Patrick J's father has been referred to me for estate accounting and I have recently received a large estate to work on from him. Estate accounting is great. You have nine months to file the returns after the date of death. If you need more time, you can get a six-month extension, but must send in the estimated tax with the extension request. The client is dead and the beneficiaries are getting money they may or may not have known they were going to receive. Therefore, there have not been many objections to the fee charged by the attorney and myself.

After I became an accountant, I thought about going to law school to become a lawyer. I thought better of it and assumed that I might obtain clients from attorneys but they would not refer any if they knew I was a lawyer. My theory really did not bear fruit until recently. Of course, the attorney fees for the estates are usually four or five times my fee.

Pat Wynne recommended Father Ryan to me. To date I have not met him. We speak on the phone and he calls me Mr. G. He is in his early 90s and I have to walk him slowly through the list of things I want him to send me annually to prepare his tax return. He is just charming and he personally pays for the education for one or two young men He is still active as a priest at a church in the Bronx.

I seem to have attracted a number of women who are either widowed or who have never married. Leslie Y is an art historian, Melinda B is a successful author who has written books and short stories that have appeared in the New York Times and other magazines, Regina R a literary agent and Patti R who runs a successful business of selling high priced ladies clothing from renown manufacturers at discount prices.

Another lady, Sandra P is currently retired but was a successful lady in her own right. I started preparing her tax returns several years ago. She had a partner, Patty G who unfortunately died of cancer a few years ago. I did not prepare the tax returns for Ms. G. When she passed away several people must have gotten together to arrange a memorial service for her. Out of deference to Sandra and because I desired to go to the memorial, I attended the service. It was held at a private club in mid Manhattan. Somewhere between 100 and 200 people were in attendance. I bumped into the gentleman who had been her accountant and we had a discussion about her claim to fame. Several people delivered eulogies and memories of being associated with Ms. G. The last of the speakers was Lily Tomlin. She spoke for about twenty minutes in glowing terms of how Ms. G. had been the cause of her success and how she owed her entire career to the lady they were honoring.

The Food Makes The Work Worthwhile.

I had as a client a used car dealer on Northern Boulevard in Woodside Queens. I looked forward to going to this client on a quarterly basis solely for the lunch. Eric M.'s mother lived in the neighborhood. When I first got them as a client I used to work at the car dealer's office, but it was not particularly pleasant to work there. It was cold in the winter and hot in the summer. I began to work at the mother's house. When Mrs. M. knew I would be coming she would prepare a pot roast that was out of this world. Eric looked forward to me coming because that way he could enjoy the same food, which Mrs. M. only made when I was there.

Eric's father had started the business. Otto M. whom I never met was a very astute man. He purchased the land at the Woodside lot and also had purchased land in Flushing, Queens, which was rented. Eric and his wife Elaine M have three sons, but none of them were interested in going into the used car business. Eric loved what he was doing and he was good at it. His mother was the bookkeeper and she was fabulous. I would prepare on a quarterly basis a financial report for her and Eric. She had already in her own method prepared a financial report in her mind. Rarely did my figures agree with hers. Sometimes her figures were more accurate than mine, but most of the time I had to show her what entries and adjustments I had and we reconciled the differences between her profits or losses and mine. It was a fascinating session and it went on every three months like clockwork.

Eric's mother Erna passed away and the house was sold. Eric's wife took over the bookkeeping and did an admirable job. Eric and I had always suggested to his mother that she allow Elaine to help more with the bookkeeping, but she was always of the opinion, and rightly so, she said that by the time I tell Elaine what to do, I will have finished it myself.

Taco Bell came along with an offer that Eric could not refuse. Eric closed the doors of the used car business, sold off the entire inventory and retired to life of a landlord. He now was collecting rents from the Flushing and Woodside properties. He continues on as a worthy friend and client.

The number of clients that I service now has substantially diminished to the point whereby I do not have to work an entire week to service the clients I still have. It suits my purpose, because I love to spend time at my home in the Hamptons. If I had retained all the clients I have serviced over the years, and they had not gone out of business or left me, I would have had a much larger practice.

Charles S. the attorney called me just over a month ago and wanted to know if I was taking on any new clients. I told him that it depends. A neighbor of his is in need of an accountant and could I please go to see him. The business is in the Bronx, and since I am an old Bronx boy, I agreed to call him. I did call him and arranged to meet with him. It is a glass business similar to James' glass business but on a much larger scale. The owner had just bought out his brother. He was paying him for the half of the business his brother owned and had already paid him for half of the real estate. An attorney, who apparently had never dealt with the sale of an interest in a business and had simply copied some paragraphs from some stock contracts, had represented him. His accountant was no better and he had gotten the raw end of a terrible deal. He had personally purchased his brother's stock certificates so that he was paying for his brother's interest with after tax dollars and it was killing him.

I have been involved, over the years, with these types of sales and I have always seen to it that the seller has some of the selling price come to him in the form of salary or consulting fee to help the buyer shoulder the burden. In addition some portion of the selling price should be attributable to goodwill, which would be written off as a tax deduction over a period of time. Some portion could be attributed to fixed assets, this would require sales tax to be submitted to the state, but would give the buyer depreciation deductions. None of this was done in this deal. Fortunately, the attorney who drew up the contract must have found a paragraph in his book of contracts that states that the buyer could assign the contract to the corporation. I am certain that the attorney never intended to put this into the contract to aid the buyer, but merely copied another paragraph from what he was using as a guide.

I decided to take him on as a client and try to straighten out the situation somewhat. I have entered the total sales price as a liability of the corporation and have given the buyer credit for the personal payments he has made to date. In addition, I have made an entry for what I deem to be a fair amount for the purchase of goodwill.

The client has supplied me with copies of the corporate and personal tax returns the accountant had prepared for them. There is absolutely no resemblance between the 2008 books and the 2008 tax returns prepared by the accountant. I called her and requested that she send me a copy of her work papers so that I can reconcile the differences. She told me that she was owed some money. I reminded her that the ethics of our profession require her to furnish me with copies of her work papers regardless of any monies due her. She said she knows about the ethics but led me to believe she will not comply with my request until she gets paid. I told the client to work it out with her because I would spend more time trying to reconcile the differences than it was worth. We will see what happens. The accountant is a mature woman who I suspect is not a CPA. Not that a failure to pass the CPA exam makes one a bad accountant. However, just looking at the corporate tax returns shows me that she is not doing a good job. She is having the corporation file on a cash basis. Which means to the layman that the corporation reports only what it has collected as income and can only deduct those expenses it has already paid. The tax law is that if a company has inventory, it must report on an accrual basis and obviously this corporation has inventory.

In addition, this woman deducted in the tax return an amount for "bad debts" in the amount of $16,000. A company, corporation or individual reporting on a cash basis cannot have a deduction for "bad debts". I know that it drives our doctor clients crazy, when we tell them that they cannot deduct on their tax returns the fees that they charge their patients and who never pay their invoices. If you are a "cash basis" operation then there is no provision to deduct for things that you have done or sold, for which you have not been paid. An accrual basis operation reports all the sales, those for which they been paid and also the accounts receivable. So that when a customer does not pay the invoice, you reverse the sale you reported, and paid tax on it, by calling it a "bad debt."

I am hoping my client comes to terms with the woman accountant soon, so that I can proceed with my regular work.

My Brother In Law Carries On.

My sister died at the age of 42. She had scarlet fever as a young teenager and it affected her heart. She had been hospitalized for her heart condition but to no avail. She was having a cup of tea in her kitchen with a neighbor, fell to the floor and she was dead. The neighbor called my brother in law and my wife. Frances called my office to obtain the telephone number where I was working and then called me. The neighbor had not told Frances that my sister was dead, but Frances feared the worst and drove to the Bronx. It was February 12th, Lincoln's birthday and I was working at Madero Silks. They were located at Madison and 32nd Street. I got on the subway and headed for my sister's apartment. I was now the sole survivor of my family. My mother had died of cancer a few years earlier. My father was still alive, but he had left our home when I was 6 years old and I had next to nothing to do with him.

My brother in law, Julius, is nine years older than me. He has been more of a father than an older brother to me. We both went into the army in 1943; both served in Europe, and arrived home safely in 1946.

Julie, whom I always called "Boss", was a very good-looking, man with red hair. His political views need much to be desired. He is Archie

Bunker personified, but he is a good decent man. He drove a truck all his life. He even goes so far back, that he began with driving a horse and wagon. When he went in service, they made him a driver of what was called a half-track in an anti aircraft outfit.

Julie worked for the same trucking company all his life. He was a union member and when he retired he went to the union headquarters to apply for his pension. The union told him that he was not entitled to any pension because his employer had never contributed on his behalf to the union' pension plan. Why the union had never advised him of this shortfall is beyond all understanding. My sister was devastated that they could not do anything to his employer or the union.

When my sister died, she left Julius with two sons to raise. They had a third son, who was born with a micro cephalic brain, which is an abnormally small brain. He lived at Willowbrook. My sister had kept him at home for the first three years of his life, but could not continue to care for him.

Julius met a woman, who was a widow and had a couple of children of her own. Sometime after they were married for a few years, they received a notice from the Internal Revenue Service notifying them that his wife, Ruth Weinberg, has not reported several thousand dollars in interest on their tax returns. Obviously, I was the one who had prepared their tax returns. I told Julius that obviously he had married a very wealthy woman, who was holding out on him. I was kidding, but there was a problem that had to be resolved. The interest had been earned from banks in Florida.

I wrote to the Internal Revenue and told them that they were mistaken and that the interest income was not hers and to correct their records. It took many months and several letters to finally resolve the problem. What had occurred, believe it not, there are two Ruth Weinbergs with the same Social Security numbers. One of them must have applied for a social security number and the Internal Revenue, with its infinite wisdom, must have assumed that it was a duplicate application and gave the second applicant the number of the first to apply.

When Julius could not retire with a reasonable pension and social security, he went back to work. The owner of the trucking company had died and Julius went into business with the owner's son. We became the accountants for the trucking company. They would pick up bales of piece goods at the New York piers and deliver them to the garment center. Again, the diminishing garment center had a disastrous effect on their business and eventually that had to close their doors. At this writing Julius is 95 years and has stated the usual quip that if her knew was going to live this long, he would have taken better care of his body.

A Client Believes The Only Way To Obtain Business Is To Offer Bribes.

Another of my clients, who never went to jail, but who perhaps should have been given a prison term was William. He created his own business of selling gift items to major corporations. These gifts were to be used for the winners of sales competition contests and other corporate purposes. William always worked on the philosophy that in order to do business with these major corporations; he would have to locate the purchasing agent who would take a bribe. I do not know how his conversations went with these people but bribes they took, in the form of television sets, refrigerators, air conditioners and cash for summer camp for their children. It always amazed me that he was always successful in finding these crooks. He was married to a lovely woman and he came home one day to find that his wife no longer loved him and threw him out of the apartment. Perhaps, she found out how he conducted his business or maybe she fell in love with someone else. William was devastated but he found another wealthy widow and married her. His business failed after a few years and I lost track of him. We bumped into each other in the Hamptons a few years ago and he had lost all his hair on his head and face from some malady. He was still trying to scheme and dream his way into making his fortune.

Public Relations Firm Enters Our Clientele Family.

Charlotte and Frank T. were partners in a public relations business. I had met Charlotte when she was employed as the chief executive of the Father's Day Council. The Council was a client of my boss. Everyone knew about Mother's Day, but Father's Day came second best. The

Council was formed to advance the promotion of Father's Day. Members consisted mainly of men's clothing and accessories manufacturers who paid annual dues. Charlotte and an assistant ran the show. Since my boss was so well established in the men's neckwear field, they became the accountants for the Council and I handled the account. Charlotte was a lady in her 50s and she was gorgeous, extremely well groomed and knew how to produce results for the Council.

Charlotte eventually left the Council and it fell apart. She and her husband opened their own public relations firm. Frank had been a reporter for the New York Times. They operated out of their apartment on 55th Street and Seventh Avenue. Charlotte called me to be her accountant and I was pleased to help. They developed a small successful firm and had Johnson and Murphy shoes and a few other prominent firms as clients. They were clients for many years. One day while I was working in my office on 57th Street, I got a call from Frank. I asked where was he calling from? He told me that he was in jail. He had gotten arrested for relieving himself in the elevator in his apartment building. Frank could not understand why they had arrested him, when dogs do it all the time. He wanted me to come to jail and get him out. I told him I would do what I could. I immediately called Charlotte and she told me that Frank had fallen off the wagon, gone on a drunken binge and that I should ignore his call. In all the years that I had known both of them, I never knew that Frank was a drunk. Eventually Frank got out of jail, but he and Charlotte drifted apart. She told me that she had it with Frank and his drinking. They separated and I never heard from him again. Soon after, Charlotte told me that Frank had died. The business fell apart because Charlotte no longer had her heart in it. They had never been wealthy people and Charlotte's finances went from bad to worse. They had never gotten divorced and since they were both well over 65 years of age, they were both collecting Social Security checks. Charlotte told me that she never notified Social Security of Frank's demise and she continued to collect both checks. I told her that she could get into a lot of trouble, but she said, "What can they do to me? If I do not get the Social Security checks, I will have to go on welfare." I heard from Claire G., the lady who always worked for Charlotte that she passed away soon thereafter

An Interesting Interview.

I have been interviewed by all kinds of people in my attempt to expand my accounting practice. One of my clients told me after he had interviewed me, that if I were as good an accountant as I am a salesman, he would be happy. The one interview that was most memorable and the one that sticks in my mind was the one with the president of a large manufacturer of ladies bras. I was given the lead and went to see this gentleman in his large, well appointed office in New York. We were partly through the interview, when he asked to be excused because he had to use the men's room. I sat in front of his desk about ten minutes waiting for him to return. The phone on his desk started to ring. I ignored the ringing since I assumed the call was for him and his secretary would get the call. The ringing persisted and eventually I got up to answer the phone to tell the person on the other end that the man they wanted to speak to was not available. But, the person on the other end of the phone was the man who was interviewing me. He was calling from his private toilet. He told me that he had this illness that required him to spend a good portion of every day in the bathroom and that we should continue our meeting. Needless to say, it was a little strange.

He engaged me to prepare his personal tax returns. His company was listed on the stock exchange and they used a nationwide accounting firm. The relationship only lasted a few years. As had always happened, when a client starts divorce proceeding, you can almost feel certain that you are going to lose them as a client. The usual chain of events is as follows. The wife calls to ask for copies of the tax returns. You tell her that you will be glad to supply them as soon as her husband gives you permission. She hangs up. You call the husband to notify him of the call. He says, "Give her nothing." Her attorney calls wanting the copies of the tax returns for the past 20 years and all other pertinent records. You tell him to call the husband's attorney and have him give you permission to release the records. The husband's attorney calls and tell you that unless you get a subpoena, give the attorney nothing. This goes back and forth and usually the wife and the husband begin to get annoyed with you. In this instance, the husband and the wife reconciled their differences and called off the divorce. Of course, the wife insisted they change accountants.

Once when I was in his office, he offered to give me a few bras for my wife. I told him that I appreciated the offer but my wife does not wear cheap brassieres. He got a little irate and said, "They are inexpensive, not cheap." I said that I stand corrected and never made that mistake again.

One Of My Eleemosynary Clients

.Michael J., a member of our small congregation in the Hamptons is a consultant to philanthropic organizations. About three years ago he came to me and inquired if I would be interested in getting an interview with a charitable organization in New York. I was interested and he gave me the telephone number of the president of the organization. He said he would call ahead so that my call would be expected.

I spoke on the phone with the president. They were currently using one of the major accounting firms in New York. They felt that they were not being treated satisfactorily; they were filing their tax reports late and had received some penalty notices. The organization, of which Mr. T. was the president, was a charitable organization that raised funds for a school in Israel. A rabbi in Israel had founded the school 35 years ago. He had taken in small children from broken homes, abused and neglected and in some case orphans. He also took in children from the street that were drug addicted and possibly in trouble with the law. The rabbi and his wife have dedicated their lives to this project. From their humble beginnings the school has grown to house about 6,000 boys and girls. They had built schoolrooms, dormitories, athletic facilities and of course a synagogue. Over and above the children who live on the premises, many more come for an education on a daily basis.

The name of the organization is American Friends of Migdal Ohr. Its sole purpose is to raise funds for the school in Israel. I told the president that I have another "American Friends" organization that raises funds for a place in Jerusalem where they serve the poor elderly by providing them with a place to come to on a daily basis where they do meaningful work, such as repairing books, shoes, furniture and other things.

After speaking on the phone and meeting the president personally, I was engaged to annually audit their books. They notified their current accountants that they were making a change and that I would be contacting them. I called for an appointment to obtain a copy of their working papers. Of course the accounting firm was paperless and I had to obtain printouts of what was contained n their laptop computers. I spent about two hours with the man who was in charge of the audit and then thanked him for his cooperation.

Our accounting industry requires ethically that when we lose a client that we assist the new accounting firm with all the records they require. When I began work on the first audit, the bookkeeper told me that she had received an invoice for the time I have spent with the accountant for the former firm. I instructed her not to pay the bill under any circumstance. I have lost clients, as previously mentioned, and I have never sent an invoice for the time I spent to supply the new accountant with any copies of my records they require.

The work at the American Friends of Migdal Ohr is interesting and I feel rewarding. One of the organizations that monitor eleemosynary organizations is Charity Navigator. They rate charitable organizations and many philanthropic persons or organizations rely on them to review and express a rating on charitable organizations. To obtain a 4 rating is the epitome of efficiency and something all charitable organizations strive for. Ever since I have been working for American Friends, they have received a 4 rating. However, with the decline in the economy, they may not be able to maintain that rating.

Technology Takes Its Toll.

Technology is a wonderful thing and obviously has helped many industries. But, technology was devastating for one of my clients. The father of one of our neighbors when we lived in Flushing had a small business. The company purchased much of the scrap tobacco and floor sweepings from all the major cigarette manufacturers in the United States. The tobacco would arrive by freight train to the Brooklyn rail yards. Trucks would then deliver the bales of tobacco to the plant. My client would have his employees run the tobacco through a series of sifters. The end products would be pipe tobacco, fertilizer and some other products. One of the cigarette manufacturers developed a system whereby they emulsified the scrap tobacco and produced a sheet of tobacco. The sheet was then sold to manufacturers of inexpensive cigars to be used as the outside wrapper. Overnight my client was out of business. He could not buy a pound of scrap tobacco. Technology had destroyed his livelihood.

Thank Heaven For Some Of My Clients.

My client Ellen Lockwood had a showroom in the garment center. She had been an executive with a large cosmetic firm and had retired. She could not stay at home and was selling products manufactured from all over the world.

Ellen reached the age of 65 and I told her to apply for Social Security benefits. She refused and did not want to lower herself to accept the payments. I finally got her to realize that she was entitled to the monthly payments and had been paying into the system for many years. She applied and was quickly turned down since she was still running her business. I submitted her tax returns showing that she was not earning very much and only continued being in business to keep busy. She chose not to pursue it. After eight years, I made her apply again because now they could not turn her down request. I went with her to the Social Security office and we met with a pleasant young man. I told him what had transpired previously. He suggested that I submit to him all the facts and documentation. Ellen received about $10,000 in back payments based on the endeavors of this young man.

Ellen represented a woman who manufactured calico clothing. The garments were kind of unique and attractive. She owned some property in Brookfield Center, Connecticut. The village was kind of a suburb of Hartford. At a sizeable expense, she converted the barn to a sewing factory and employed some of the local women to cut and sew the fabric. She came up with the idea of creating a woman's calico raincoat. It required that the calico fabric be adhered to plastic sheeting. She never quite got it right and eventually had to abandon the idea.

About the time I was acting as her accountant, we ran into a serious problem at home. My middle daughter Amy woke one morning and told us that she was in pain and could not walk. She was about four years old at the time. We immediately took her to our doctor and he recommended a specialist. We made an appointment and went to see him as soon as we could. He took some x rays and examined her extensively. He told us that Amy had osteocondritis, which was a flattening of her hip socket and that she would never walk properly again. Obviously, we were devastated.

Mrs. G. who owned the calico factory was married to a doctor. He was reputed to have invented the glue that adheres the bag to the body after a person has a colostomy. I was at their brownstone in New York reviewing her records and I mentioned to him Amy's condition. He did not say a word to me but went to the phone. He dialed a number and he said, "Walter this is Ted. I am sending my accountant, his wife and his daughter to see you right now." It turned out the Doctor Ted G. and Dr. Walter C. had shared an office several years prior to this telephone conversation. They had parted ways in an unfriendly situation and had not spoken in years.

Dr. Walter C. saw us that very afternoon. We told him of the diagnosis we had received from this other doctor. He took his own x rays and must have spent the better part of two hours examining Amy. At the end of his examination he told us to put Amy to bed for a couple of days and that she would be right as rain by then. Connections, connections, connections. I did not know how to thank Doctor Ted G. for going out of his way to help us.

How To Be Seen

I have had many other clients in a variety of industries. I was never able to expand my practice to the point where I had to hire staff. My partner Fred and I handled all our clients and occasionally hired per diem assistants. I do not belong to a country club and I do not play golf. I have not spent a great deal of time entertaining and soliciting clients. The new clients I obtained came from recommendations from current clients, friends, attorneys and occasionally a banker. I have no regrets. With the clientele that I assembled, I have been able to support my family reasonable well, send my three daughters to the finest colleges and assist with sending my grandchildren to the finest colleges as well.

My oldest daughter graduated Phi Beta Kappa from Brandeis University, obtained her Masters in English from Columbia University. She worked for a while at a major publishing company and became permissions editor. Her job entailed working with lawyers and soon thereafter decided to become an attorney. She then went on to Harvard University to obtain her law degree. My middle daughter works for us on a part time basis. She too, had attended Brandeis University for two years and then wanted to pursue a mathematical career and switched to the University of Pennsylvania to obtain her bachelor degree. From there she went on to Dartmouth to obtain her Master's Degree and subsequently became a Certified Public Accountant. Our youngest daughter began her college career at Albany College, left there after two years and completed her college education at Clark University. She worked for a company that rented photo images of world famous photographers and became the manager of their library. Another company bought them and she left to pursue a cooking career. She became a "personal chef" for wealthy people. She shopped for them and cooked an entire week's meals.

My grandson won a four-year scholarship to Tulane University, but decided to go to the University of Pennsylvania instead. He graduated from there and went on to Albert Einstein Medical School. He recently graduated and is doing his internship at Montefiore's Children's Hospital. His desire is to become a pediatrician. He married his childhood sweetheart Faith a month after his graduation His younger sister followed in the footsteps of her mother and brother and graduated from the University of Pennsylvania and is currently getting her master's degree from Columbia . . .

People keep asking me when I plan on retiring. I still have my health and my brain is still functioning and at this time, I have no plans to retire. About ten years ago we were forced to move from our office. The tenant sharing the floor with us gave our landlord an ultimatum. He wanted the entire floor or he would move. Out lease had come to an end and we moved. After we found our current space, we mailed announcement cards notifying everyone of our new address. I received some hysterical phone calls from clients. They thought that I was announcing my retirement. I enjoy what I do and cannot envision sitting home and doing nothing.

Enjoying my work as I do, when I look at my watch and see that it is 4 o'clock in the afternoon, my thoughts are usually that my gosh it is already 4 PM. Whereas many working people would say that my gosh it is only 4 PM.

Whenever any of my clients are subject to an examination by the Internal Revenue or any other taxing authority, during the course of the exam I always ask the examiner how many years they have been working on this job. The answer is always, "I have four years to go or I have sixteen years to go." The mentality is always the same that they are serving out their sentence and will begin to enjoy life once they have retired and are collecting their pension.

My wife and I have traveled extensively and have seen many parts of the globe. We do not look forward to extended airplane flights at this point in our lives. I have only a few business clients left in my practice and I enjoy servicing them. They have all pleaded with me not to retire. Other than the tax season, when I still work full time and most Saturdays, I am able to limit my workweek to about three days a week. We purchased a home in the Hamptons over 25 years ago. We love it there and spend as much time as possible out there.

If I had the proper guidance before writing this book, someone might have told me to make an outline of what I wanted to include. If I had done that, then the sequence of events would have been in chronologically order. However I have written about my experiences as they popped into my head and the results are what you have just read.

Many of my accounting friends have already retired and seem to be enjoying themselves. The day may come soon when I will be forced to retire because of health, but for the time being, as long as I still do not find accounting boring, I will keep practicing. Maybe someday I will get it right,